Praise for *F**k It* and John C. Parkin

'*Stressed, angry or upset? Then try F**k It therapy.*'
SUNDAY TIMES STYLE

'*Everyone can relate to F**k It.*'
THE TIMES

'*John combines Wayne Hemingway's style with Eddie Izzard's flights of surrealism.*'
THE GUARDIAN

'*The self-help phenomenon that we can all swear by.*'
EVENING STANDARD

'*"F**k It". I was practising the words. They rolled around my head. We need to say "F**k It" when we're out of sync with the natural world; it helps us go with the flow.*'
THE OBSERVER

'*This book makes me smile and, more importantly, clicks my brain into positive mode.*'
FEARNE COTTON

'*This brilliant, funny, wise book gives us the kick we need to stop making excuses and do what we love. Parkin is living proof that it can be done.*'
METRO UK

'*A new life bible urging us to tip the life balance back in our direction and make time for what's important, rather than all that stuff we feel we should be doing.*'
SUNDAY MIRROR

f**k it

BE AT PEACE
WITH LIFE
JUST AS IT IS

Also by John C. Parkin

Books

F**k It – Do What You Love (2016)

F**k It Is the Answer (2014)

F**k It: The Ultimate Spiritual Way (2008, 2014)

F**k It Therapy (2012)

The Way of F**k It (2009)

Audiobooks

F**k It Therapy (2015)

F**k It: The Ultimate Spiritual Way (2014)

The F**k It Show (2010)

f★★k it

BE AT PEACE
WITH LIFE
JUST AS IT IS

John C. Parkin

HAY HOUSE
Carlsbad, California • New York City
London • Sydney • New Delhi

Library of Congress Control Number: 2018938601

Tradepaper ISBN: 978-1-4019-5571-7

16 15 14 13 12 11 10 9 8 7
1st edition, June 2018

Printed in the United States of America

CONTENTS

CONTENTS

WELCOME TO
THE GAME OF LIFE

If you're anything like me, you'll have read through the 'contents' of this book to see what's in store for you. Actually, if you're anything like me, you may well have read them in the bookshop, to see if it was worth buying the book.

Because you can tell a lot from a contents list; in fact, you can tell so much from a contents list that sometimes it's enough just to read that – you get the feeling you won't glean that much more by spending multiple hours (depending on your reading speed) reading the details between the chapter titles that constitute the full book.

So, the first part of my job, really, over the course of this book, is to persuade you that it was worth going beyond the 'contents'. The second part is to get you from Level 1 to Level 3. And I'd suggest that reading the contents alone will not get you to Level 3.

I said 'if you're anything like me', and that of course implies that some of you haven't yet read the contents. You've dived in recklessly, with no thought for the context of what you're reading. Did you even see the title of the book? Or did a good friend who was concerned for your welfare give you the book, and you didn't really look at it; instead, going on trust, you just got stuck into the introduction?

Actually, I suspect there are even some readers who'll ignore the introduction and go straight to the first chapter. I can say anything about them here because they're never going to read it. They don't read the chapter titles and they don't read the introduction. Fools.

They'll never get to Level 3, as getting there takes a level of incisive intelligence – along with other qualities like patience and self-awareness (which aren't necessarily subsets of intelligence, as I know plenty of intelligent but impatient and self-ignorant people).

The point I'm making here is about the 'game' structure I've chosen for the book – this Level 1, 2, 3 thing. I like a good game, especially at Christmas: a parlour game, or a board game, or even a video game (if I can manage to get my hands on a controller).

Actually, I've been known to pay my children for a go on their video games. I say 'their' rather generously of course, because I paid my hard-earned cash for both the hardware and the various overpriced pieces of software, the 'games'. So having to then pay a further sum to actually play the game does seem rather unfair. Hey-ho.

And this 'level' thing is more like a video game. It's rather flippant, of course, to suggest that 'life is a game'. For most people, for most of the time, life doesn't feel like much of a game: it feels difficult and stressful. But part of getting to Level 3 is becoming aware that there's a game-like quality to life. Which makes life more like a game that everyone is forced to play, without knowing it's a game; it's only revealed to be a game if you get to the highest level.

All analogies fall down, of course, upon scrutiny. Look at the Old Testament, for example.

HOW THIS BOOK CAME ABOUT

During a F**k It Weekend I was running earlier this year, I had a realization: there's another level to the F**k It concept – one that's beyond what I'd previously imagined. This realization sent me on a journey of discovery (this book) that manifested in rather astonishing shifts in perspective. And if you read this book slowly, and ponder it sufficiently, and follow some of the suggestions it contains, and give it enough time, with a good wind, you too will experience similar (or dissimilar, but still astonishing) shifts in perspective.

I can't guarantee that, of course. There's no money-back guarantee of Level 3 enlightenment here. But I'm holding nothing back: I've seen some light, and I've worked out how to keep seeing the light. And I'm sufficiently good at describing the light – as well as explaining how *you* can see it and *keep* seeing it – so I don't think I'd have to shell out that much cash if there *were* a money-back guarantee (and you could persuade me that although you'd done your part, the light still wasn't being seen).

So, back to that realization I had on the F**k It Weekend: it both blew me away with its power and pissed me off – because it kind of undermined the whole point of the weekend. I also knew that, to understand this realization fully, and to absorb it into my life and my way of being, I'd have to investigate it, unpack it, live it, and see what popped up through that investigation.

The title of the weekend was 'Be More F**k It', and early on, the participants and I listed all the aspects of our behaviour and personality that are *not* so 'F**k It'. So people noted things like: 'take things too seriously', 'uptight', 'thin-skinned', 'over-ambitious', 'quick to anger', 'judgemental', 'stressed', 'care too much about what others think', 'afraid', and so on.

Then we looked at what, for us, would constitute being *more* F**k It. Here, people listed things like: 'relaxed', 'open', 'happy', 'not so bothered about what others think', 'content in my own skin', 'patient', 'optimistic', 'courageous', 'light-hearted', and so on.

I wrote up these suggestions on two flipcharts and we all looked at the two lists – less F**k It and more F**k It. And then I suddenly realized something. I asked the group: 'Can you think of some prominent people in the world who personify these qualities?' The response was immediate: 'Trump and Obama'. And it was very striking. Trump was the personification of 'less F**k It', as the participants had defined it for themselves, and Obama was completely 'F**k It'.

Granted, this was in the early days of Trump's presidency, so he was naturally top of our minds then (as he is now, too). But the list of 'less F**k It' qualities did describe him to a 'T' for 'Trump'. Although another possible view of the orange one is that he's actually rather 'F**k It' – in his straight-talking, shoot-from-the-hip, make-it-up-as-he-goes-along way.

And the more F**k It list did describe Obama – or 'No-Drama Obama' as his colleagues in the White House referred to him. In fact, when I saw a particular photo of him – taken in February 2017, when many of us were worrying ourselves sick about what Trump would say or do next – Obama's F**kitness bothered even me: he was on a boat with Richard Branson, wearing a wetsuit – having just been kitesurfing – and looking as if he didn't have a care in the world.

So, having established what constitutes less or more F**k It in our lives, I wanted to use a technique called 'muscle testing' to evaluate these qualities. Muscle testing is the ability to gauge how strong you are, based on certain conditions; for example, it's often used to test for allergies. I like to use it to compare the effect on our bodies of certain thoughts or states.

Muscle testing is easy to do: you stand up straight, raise one arm out to your side and then make a statement out loud; a person standing directly behind you then tries to push down your arm while you resist the pressure (see the drawing below).

Muscle testing

The first 'muscle test' I usually do is a person's name: they say their own name out loud, followed by an invented name. They discover (usually) that their arm is stronger (i.e. it resists the pressure more) when they say their own name.

The F**k It Weekend group and I set about testing less and more F**k It. Each person chose a sentence that summed up a less F**k It aspect of themselves – for example, 'I'm really impatient.' They said this sentence out loud as another person tested the strength of their outstretched arm. After this, they tested a more F**k It version of the same thing (though it had to be believable). So: 'I know that, sometimes, things need to happen at their own pace.'

Now, truth matters in muscle testing (as the testing of the person's real name demonstrates), so the more F**k It assertion had to draw on some truth within the person. And, in this example, most impatient people can see that things *do* need to happen at their own pace sometimes.

With the group organized into pairs, the testing took place. And, generally, people found that they were physically stronger when asserting the *more* F**k It sentence.

After this exercise there was a question from one of the group, so I invited her out to the front, to test her myself. She was, indeed, stronger with the more F**k It assertion. Job done. I could have let her sit down, but there was something wrong. Even though she was happy with the result – and couldn't believe how much stronger she'd been when giving herself permission to be more F**k It – I still felt there was something wrong.

As the woman started to return to her seat, I called her back, and asked her to test *a new sentence*. Now, I'll tell you *what* she was testing, but I won't tell you *who* she was. So I'll call her 'Judi Dench'. (Of course, it wasn't *actually* Judi Dench – that's just a name I've given her. She was nothing like Judi Dench, and neither did her name begin with 'M'.)

So Judi Dench's 'less F★★k It' sentence was: 'I care too much what others think of me.' ('Well, maybe you shouldn't have become an actor then, eh, Dame Judi?' you might say.) And her 'more F★★k It' sentence was: 'I don't care *so* much about what others think of me.' Which was believable and possible for her, so it made her stronger.

The new sentence I asked her to test was this: 'On occasion, it's perfectly natural to be bothered about what others think of me.' She began repeating this new sentence, and raised her arm ready for me to test her (for a third time). I pressed down on her arm – slowly at first, as we teach people to do, then more forcefully – and I couldn't budge it an inch. Judi Dench was rock solid. Again, she couldn't believe it.

THE THIRD LEVEL TO F★★K IT

But this time she was confused: wasn't the point of the exercise to see how 'being more F★★k It' was the answer? In fact, wasn't *that* the point of the whole weekend? Well, yes it was. But my definition of what 'being more F**k It' means was being tested itself. I felt exhilarated though, as I knew this was a big insight for us all.

I knew then that there was a *third level* to this F**k It thing. In Dame Judi's case:

Level 1: I stress about what others think of me, and that blocks me and bothers me.

Level 2: I find a way to be not so bothered about what others think of me.

Level 3: I realize that it's fine to be stressed about what others think of me occasionally, as it's perfectly natural.

And in our case, when we apply Level 3 to the subject of being at peace – which is what this book's about, after all – it goes something like this:

Level 1: I'm stressed and don't feel peaceful.

Level 2: I find ways to feel peaceful.

Level 3: I'm at peace with being stressed at times and peaceful at others, as *both* are a natural part of life.

Now that might be confusing you as you read it (as it confused Judi Dench and the rest of the group on that 'Be More F**k It' workshop). If so, relax: there's a whole book here for us to explore this.

Or you might instead feel a blast of freedom as you realize what this book has to offer. The doorway to this understanding is 'F**k It'. Saying 'F**k It to being peaceful' can easily confuse you (if being 'at peace' is what you're after – and, having bought the book, there's a good chance that it is), but it can also offer a glimmer of the freedom to come when you start to care less about things; even the very things you most want.

So, please say after me: 'I know I want it, but F**k It to being peaceful.' And let's go explore this new game of life some more.

LEVEL 1

I'LL BE AT PEACE WHEN...

Although we're just starting out, at Level 1, we're pretty advanced in the sussing-out-life game if we believe that 'being at peace' is an important aim. You may already have reached this level, even though you might have used expressions such as 'I'll be fine when...' or 'I'll be happy when...' instead of 'I'll be at peace when...'.

The sub-Level 1 strata are made up of more or less unconscious scramblings through life. We go after jobs because that's what we're supposed to do. We take up offers simply because they're offered – regardless of whether or not they're good for us.

We get closer to Level 1 when we understand that we do most things, and aim at most things, in order to *feel* something in particular. When we're young, that thing might be 'excitement' or 'a thrill'. As we mature, it might be 'relaxation' or 'contentment'.

I've settled on this 'at peace' thing because I think it's what's there *underneath* for most of us. I don't need to be excited all the time, or relaxed all the time, or happy all the time, but to be 'at peace' all the time feels like a high aim to have.

So, as you read through this Level 1 section, you might occasionally need to substitute the 'at peace' bit for something similar. As a child I would have said 'I'll be happy [rather than at peace] when I get a Raleigh Chopper'; but it was being at peace that I wanted, even then, even if I didn't know it.

I'LL BE AT PEACE WHEN... I GET A RALEIGH CHOPPER

Do you know what a Raleigh Chopper is? It's the best bike ever invented: with a seat like a Yamaha motorbike, a gearstick on the crossbar straight out of a Ford Mustang, handlebars from a Harley Davidson and a name from a Western.

And I wanted one. I went to sleep every night imagining what it would be like to own one. I knew that I'd be happy, and that my life would be complete, if I could just have a Chopper.

I know this is a funny one to start on, but I'll never know whether I'd have been forever happy, and my life complete, because I never got that Chopper. Instead, I got a Grifter. I can't remember why. It wasn't due to my parents' lack of generosity – maybe the shop was out of Choppers.

Maybe I need to buy one now, eh? Maybe a Chopper is *still* the answer?

Fortunately, though, we all have other things in our lives – things that we want, and then succeed in getting – and through these we'll see whether the 'at peace' outcome can be achieved as anticipated.

I'LL BE AT PEACE WHEN... THE SCHOOL HOLIDAYS ARRIVE

For me, school was long, drawn-out agony. I didn't have a 'misspent' youth – I spent much of my time diligently applying myself to my studies – but I dreaded most classes.

I spent a lot of energy either trying to slow down time – as I waited for the dreaded Monday, or a test or exam – or speed it up, longing for the breaks and the holidays. I bet time got confused. Consequently, I wished most of my teenage years away – those precious years. I wished those heavy weeks in those dark classrooms with the sadistic teachers gone – so that I could get to the holidays.

The holidays were then like escaping to a desert island, and I did find peace, of sorts. Of course, after a while I'd be looking forward to the holidays *within* the holidays – the times when the family would go away to the Lake District or the seaside. Even within the holidays within the holidays, I'd be looking forward to the more special bits.

I can recall my precise thought processes at different times of my life. And I'm somewhat reluctant to commit this to paper/screen because it both fixes it and changes it slightly. It's like taking a photograph: after a while the original memory starts to fade and you remember only the photograph. So I'm afraid that I'll only remember the words I'm about to use, rather than the original thought impressions. Hey-ho, in I go for you, reader.

For most of my childhood holidays, we went to the same seaside town on England's east coast (Sutton-on-Sea), and stayed at the same guesthouse (Holmfirth Christian Guest House), with the same relatives (grandparents and aunts and uncles), and the same 'other' family (the Roscamps from Sheffield in the north of England). And we'd do pretty much the same thing every year, only changing with the evolving habits and desires of age.

The first full day of the week (Sunday) would start with chapel. And during the service – with its quaint Methodist hymns and prayers from a bygone time, and a sermon from a blind old man called Mr Lockwood, who sounded to me just as I imagined John Wesley would have sounded – I'd be wishing I was on the beach.

But I was also aware that I shouldn't be wishing away time, as this was SUTTON-ON-SEA. And the last thing I should be doing was trying to speed up time. I'd go back and forth like that for a while.

Later, while building a sandcastle on the beach, I'd be looking forward to the big game of football we'd all have on the sand. Dads would come down to join us. Mr Roscamp had once been in the Manchester United squad. Our dad liked (and still likes) to think he was in the Aston Villa squad, though the reality was he'd been called to a trial and told 'you only have one foot'. As a child, I never understood that story, as he quite obviously had two. Maybe the coach was Mr Lockwood.

So I'd do my best to restrain my 'Ooohhh, I can't wait' impatience to get onto the next heavenly thing, and try to just enjoy what we were doing. This would now be called mindfulness exercises, and that's what I was doing – effectively saying, 'I must be present to this – it's marvellous.' It was fairly hopeless though, because, in my super-excited-kid way, I *did* want to get to the next thing.

I'LL BE AT PEACE WHEN... I'M BACK WITH MY FRIENDS

We've just returned home after our annual three-week trip to the volcanic island of Stromboli, off the north coast of Sicily (where we teach retreats). It's heaven there. Our 15-year-old twin boys love it too. But one of them, Arco, spent the last week moaning that he wanted to be back home – to 'be with my friends'.

I get it. My sister and I spent ages looking forward to being with our Sheffield friends, Andy and Joy Roscamp, every summer. Then, as the new school term neared, my dread of school was partially balanced by a desire to be back with my school friends.

You feel like yourself with your friends (if they're the right friends). You have fun with your friends. Everything will be OK when I'm back with my friends.

I'LL BE AT PEACE WHEN... I GET MY QUALIFICATIONS

When we're very young, we're naturally more 'present', aren't we? As kids, we are as most of us would like to be as adults. Not in the endlessly eating crisps and ice cream sense (that's something I still do, but would prefer not to), but in our ability to just play and be present, and not plan what we'll do for the day, or worry about things not getting done.

But as we grow up, we encounter built-in systems that turn us into left-brained (more on that later), future-facing machines. And one of those systems is exams and qualifications. God knows what it's like now in the UK (our boys have been schooled in Italy, which is blissfully free of tests and exams); if anyone starts talking about SATs or 11-plus exams or any other tests to evaluate kids' academic level, I stick my fingers in my ears and go 'la la la la' until they stop.

I took my first exam at 11 – to get into the Institute of Sadism that I attended for seven years. Although I now know what came afterwards, I do recall sitting in the exam hall, looking at the invigilating pupils in their smart blazers and thinking, *I'll be happy if I can just get in here.* So I got in (temporary relief and happiness).

Then there were two sets of exams every year: at Christmas and in summer – two words that should be all pleasantness but which were (thankfully temporarily) sullied by the presence of the exams. The exams would occasionally take on more import (for us, they were 'O' levels and 'A' levels), and the stakes got higher too.

The last lot allowed us entry into the Institute of Freedom, aka university. This was in the near-forgotten days when an 18-year-old didn't have to take out a huge loan in order to learn good stuff just for the sake of it. Stuff that would later benefit others in a variety of difficult-to-quantify ways – and also in the easier-to-quantify form of higher taxes paid to the state to support others' welfare and learning.

And thus the cycle of 'I can relax when the exams are over' started early. Of course, there was a built-in secondary trap too – like a mouse that manages to steal the cheese with only a grazed tail, the bigger vice would come clamping down in the form of 'the exam results'. Several summers were spent in blessed relief that school and exams were over, but then we'd start to feel the growing shadow of the imminent results block out the sunlight.

Like lab animals, the system trains us early to think 'I'll be at peace when...'. And it's a difficult habit to lose.

LEVEL 1 HACK

This is most likely too late for you, but don't grow up too quickly. Don't listen too much to your teachers, or even your parents in many cases. Keep playing. Keep dreaming. Don't answer when you're asked what you'll do when you grow up. Only answer when asked what you'll be doing this afternoon.

I'LL BE AT PEACE WHEN… THEY SAY 'YES'

If only they would notice me, and say 'yes' to going out; then I'd feel OK. And they would then say 'yes' to going out again, of course, and we'd become an item.

Then I hope I'd get a 'yes' to getting closer, if you know what I mean. And that there'd be lots of yes, yes, yeses from both of us. Then maybe we'd both say 'yes' to settling down together. That would be good. Then I'd be at peace.

Maybe we'd then say 'yes' to having kids, which is a whole other game, I suppose. And I just hope that they don't say 'yes' to anyone else along the way. And I hope I don't, either.

I hope that when we argue, we can say sorry and find our peace. I hope that if I'm wrong, I'll be forgiven, and find my peace. I hope that if they are wrong, I can forgive, and leave them in peace. I hope that, if it ends, we can both move on, and find our peace.

The 'circle of control' is a concept that says there are things in life that we can control (or think we can) – such as what we eat. Outside the circle of control is the 'circle of influence', where we can't fully control the outcome, but we can influence it. So this might be what our teenage son or daughter eats. Then outside that is the 'circle of concern', where we can't control the outcome, and we can't really influence it, but we're concerned about it. So this might be what children in Africa are eating, or not.

A more rational route through this question of finding our peace suggests that we should concentrate only on the things that we can control. So it would make more sense to believe we can be more at peace when we've passed our exams, than when world peace has been achieved.

On this basis, our intimate relationships – one of the most important aspects of our lives and one in which we hope to find peace – involve another party whom we cannot control, and should probably be wary of even trying to influence (although we should clearly demonstrate some concern for them).

In other words, to rely on others for your sense of peace, even your nearest and dearest, is not a particularly functional way to go about things. Sorry.

I'LL BE AT PEACE WHEN... THERE'S PEACE IN THE WORLD

I grew up in the shadow of the Cold War, with its ever-present threat of nuclear apocalypse. As I became more politically aware, I struggled to find peace within myself when there was so much struggle at the geo-political level. But then the Berlin Wall came down, Nelson Mandela was released, there was 'glasnost' in Russia, and a new kind of opening occurred around the world. And we could relax, at last.

But at the time of writing, there's uncertainty and threat everywhere: the war in Syria, the ballistic missile tests launched by North Korea, tensions around Russia, and President Trump's daily tweets. What would it take to be at peace in this environment? For the wars to end, for Kim Jong-un to halt his nuclear weapons programme, for

Putin to stop provoking Europe with military exercises, for Trump to stop tweeting?

We know that none of those things is likely to happen any time soon, but it's still difficult to find peace until they do. We sit and watch the news (well, we don't really do that anymore do we? We don't just watch it, and it isn't broadcast at a fixed time these days; instead, it bleeds into all our waking hours) and remind ourselves how absurd it would be to feel at peace now.

I'LL BE AT PEACE WHEN... I HAVE MY OWN CAR

When we're young, a car is freedom on wheels – it's the primary mode of transport for taking us out of the family home and into the outside world. From rules and restrictions to freedom, via the open road.

Can you remember the feeling of getting into your own car for the first time, then shutting the door and just driving around? There was a total thrill to doing that. I thought I'd be happy once I'd passed my driving test and owned my own car. And I did feel that way once I was out on the road.

I felt pretty relaxed and at peace in my car for the first few days and weeks. I remember driving sedately as I learned the ropes, but then something else took over. I wanted to be faster than the other road users. It wasn't enough to be driving my vehicle of freedom *with* others on the roads – I had to be driving *past* the others.

A similar thing has happened many times in my life, including with these *F**k It* books. I won't write a section title like 'I'll be at peace when... I get my book published' because it scores pretty low on the universality scale (lower even than the Chopper). So I'll bury it here, under first cars, but...

I'd written the first F**k It book (*F**k It, the Ultimate Spiritual Way*) and found an agent via a friend (hurrah!) But he couldn't find a publisher (boo!), so I decided to self-publish, which I did 10 years ago today (hurrah!) People liked the book and talked about it, and soon I received an email from Michelle Pilley, officially the Best Managing Director of the Best Mind, Body, Spirit Publisher in the World, Hay House (UK) who, after a meeting, offered to publish it (double hurrah!)

And, throughout that process, I told myself I wasn't bothered if the book was published or not. But I was only trying to protect myself from the disappointment of it not being published. I *was* bothered, because getting published felt like a very good thing indeed.

In fact, in the moments when I wasn't pretending I wasn't bothered, I do remember thinking, *Oooh, if I were published, that would be it. I could just relax, and my work would be done, because I'd be PUBLISHED.*

So the papers were signed and, even though the arrival of the finished book on bookshop shelves was still a few months off, I was now PUBLISHED, and I sat back in that feeling. And it felt as good as I'd imagined it would. My work was done. I'd made it. I was a published author.

I sat like an author (imagining myself with a pipe). I walked like an author (at a slow but confident pace). I talked like an author (preceding every sentence with a drawn-out 'Wellllll...'). I'd arrived at the summit of life. I could now sit down, relax, and gaze upon this wondrous world, oxygen permitting.

This 'at peace' (and somewhat self-satisfied) feeling lasted for a few days. Just as I drove around at a sedate pace in my newly owned (but not new) car. Then something else kicked in. I couldn't be just any old published author: I had to be a *successful* published author. So the next time I saw Michelle, I asked her, 'How many copies must the book sell for you to consider it a success?'

She mentioned a figure. It didn't sound so many. I pushed harder: 'What would be a HUGE success for you, then?' She mentioned another figure.

And I was off. My foot hit the accelerator. I could now see where the other drivers were on the road, and I wanted to pass them. I'd drop into a lower gear, my twin exhaust manifold would hum like a Lamborghini's, and I'd pass those frickin' Sunday drivers in their hats, giving them the finger as I did so.

That's what happened to the idea that I'd be at peace when I got my book published... just the same as what happened when I thought I'd be at peace when I got my own car.

I'LL BE AT PEACE WHEN... I FIND MY IDEAL JOB

When I emerged from university in the late 1980s, the UK economy was in a deep recession and the outlook for employment was grim. Signing up for income support was not the way I'd planned to start my working life, so I thought I'd be happy with *any* job.

My first (temporary) job was in the post office. I'd sort letters into the appropriate streets, ready for the postmen to pick up and deliver. And I was quite happy there for a while. Before long I'd moved onto filing and photocopying in various offices around Maidenhead, a town in southeast England; and then onto a job with some interesting prospects, in one of the offices in which I'd been filing.

But I realized, over time, that I'd like to write for a living – and I fancied the idea of writing television ads. So the journey began. It's not an easy job to get: I had to sell my car and go back to college, and then spend a year chasing my first opportunity in a good London advertising agency.

But being hungry makes you appreciative of food. In the year that my creative partner and I were tramping the streets of London, taking our portfolio to swanky agency after swanky agency (with the odd wanky agency along the way), the idea of having a desk in one of those places grew more and more appealing.

How cool would it be to be a creative in a London agency? I imagined that, once we'd got the job, my partner and I could sit back and enjoy the good life. The ideas would flow. The commercials would be made. We'd enjoy anonymous fame during the ad breaks that punctuated Britain's greatest soap operas.

The feeling of getting that first job was great; and then being hired by our dream agency was even better. That was a sit-back-and-enjoy feeling. But the peace didn't last long, as we're beginning to learn – and I couldn't settle until I'd done some great work.

Then, after the first bit of good work (the first TV commercial for Haagen Dazs), I couldn't settle until I'd done some more. You're only as good as your last ad, they say in adland. I took that a step further: I was only as good as my next ad.

And there's something else to be said here, isn't there, about the advertising business? And maybe I could add an 'of course' to this, as it may be patently obvious to you. I always saw advertising as a fun way to communicate the benefits of a product to the nation. If you don't object to free-market capitalism (and there are many who do, I know), how can you object to companies advertising their wares?

I had no moral objection to advertising in principle, though there were areas of the business that I *did* object to, and wouldn't work on (such as advertising cigarettes). But, in this book about 'being at peace with life', advertising clearly doesn't exist to make us feel at peace. It exists to sell more stuff, and we generally buy more stuff when we don't feel we have enough, or *are* enough.

The advertising world (and the corporate world it represents) doesn't want you to feel at peace with life, as it is. But then again, that's life, as it is.

I'LL BE AT PEACE WHEN... I HAVE A PLACE TO CALL HOME

An Englishman's home is his castle. I'm not sure what this means, as most castles were built as a defence against rampaging marauders, and, unless you live in particular postcodes, I can't imagine that's a priority.

We load the idea of having our own home with so much: it's a place to express our personality; a place to escape to; a place to be ourselves. And, in the UK for the last 20 years or so, it's been a place we regard as our own personal pot of gold.

My first place was a loft in East London – I'd seen too many jeans commercials in the 1980s. It wasn't a very big loft; my brother-in-law remarked that it was 'more like a pigeon loft' – he pronounced this with a northern English accent, because he's from the north of England, and therefore knows what a pigeon loft looks like. And, admittedly, it was more a narrow room with a very high ceiling. But it was in an old factory at least.

I can remember sitting in that empty, echoey space on my first night, looking around and saying to myself, *This is mine. It's MINE.* It was a very good feeling. And I was at peace there. For a while, at least (as usual).

The fact that the feeling didn't last (as usual) may be (small) comfort to the masses of young people who are struggling to afford a place of their own (or even to rent a place of their own). I'm sorry. It's not fair. Throughout my life I've enjoyed owning various properties, but it's not the ultimate answer. It won't solve everything.

But it's worth talking a little about the essentials that can be an objective and serious block to feeling any kind of peace, ever. There are some things that we just plain 'need' if we're to have any chance of a decent life and a minimum level of wellbeing – physical and mental.

For us humans, this has probably been the case for a long, long time. We have a basic survival need for shelter (a safe place to live, protected from the elements); food and water for ourselves and our families; and a way to heat ourselves and light our space. And we thus usually need a way to 'earn' these things, commonly via some form of work. For most of us, it's been a while since our ancestors built and maintained their own shelters, hunted for or grew their own food, chopped wood for heat, and so on.

But if you think about how much of the money you earn from doing some modern kind of work goes on your property, food and water, and energy bills, you'll probably realize that not a lot has changed. We've introduced an exchange mechanism so that we don't literally have to build our own shelters or produce our own food. Our properties, meals and means of keeping warm are vastly more sophisticated now, but still.

And just as the desires of our ancestors hundreds of years ago might have revolved around less gruelling work, or a more comfortable home, or a special meal, how much desire energy do you spend on thinking of better (and better paid) work, a nicer property and a fancy meal out? Given such ancient experience with the same desires and needs, how good are we at getting it?

Well, the problem is that the goalposts keep changing, don't they? One minute you're thinking you've got it all worked out, with your excellent father-passed-to-son hunting skills, and the next minute you're looking askance at the price of a ready-made crispy duck meal from some posh supermarket. One minute it's enough to get into grammar school, then choose a good, solid job that'll set you up for life. The next minute everyone's talking about portfolio jobs and the rise of the robots.

One minute you can buy a nice terraced house, fit for you and your future family, for the price of a year's earnings. The next minute, you'd have to sell your grandmother to afford the shed in the back yard of the same terraced house.

One minute you're burning coal to heat yourself and cook your food – coal that was mined in the next county and delivered by a lorry to your cellar. The next minute you're paying the price of a shed every year to a company that agrees to light your home from an unknown source – fracked gas, perhaps, or a nuclear power station, or unsightly wind farms – and passes most of the money to a shareholder who lives in the biggest house on the street.

Yet, until we get a national basic living wage for which we need to do no work in return, we'll need to find some way to earn some money to pay for the shelter, the sustenance and the heat and light.

So, because those bloody goalposts *keep changing* – unlike in the real game of football, that's kind of what the metaphorical goalposts do, isn't it? – we need to get used to being ready to shoot at a moving target.

I'LL BE AT PEACE WHEN...
WE HAVE A FAMILY

Talking of football, let's have some kids, so I can play football with them in the park.

Now, I know we don't all want a family. I have one, as you know, but I didn't for years. Sorry, it's sounding like a commodity, isn't it? 'I put up with saggy jowls for years. I know a face tuck isn't for everyone – I never imagined I'd want one, actually – but since Dr Tucker did his magic, I've never felt better.'

So for those of you who do want to have kids... We imagine that life will be complete when they arrive. And there's no overstating how totally gorgeous it is to have children. Our boys are 15 and I've spent their lives thinking something along the lines of, *Oh, this is probably the best age – appreciate this, as it'll change soon*, and I continue to do so.

Being 'Dad' is probably the most cherished bit of my spell on this planet. Whenever the boys call me 'Dad', which they do all the time (as I've banned 'John' and 'wanker'), a little bit of me melts. But… it ain't peaceful. That's the last thing it is. You know that, without me explaining it (if you don't have kids), don't you? And being at peace? Well, for the times when you feel that, there are an equal number of times when you feel the opposite.

I recognized this the very day I learned that my wife Gaia was pregnant with twins (we knew she was pregnant, but it was a trip to the hospital for a checkup that confirmed everything was OK and that there were two of them). I felt elated, and at the exact same moment I felt an entirely new feeling of responsibility. I felt the total joy of new life, combined with the huge potential for pain at the vulnerability of said life, and my responsibility for it.

I'LL BE AT PEACE WHEN... THE KIDS ARE OFF TO SCHOOL

I remember our boys' first day at nursery school, the windows of which had views onto the mountains (unlike at my schools: one of which looked onto the municipal dump, and the other, onto a caravan concession).

After dropping off the boys, Gaia and I drove back home, where it was... quiet. However you look after your kids before they go off to school – whether you share childcare, have grandparents nearby, employ a nanny, or are on your own – it's hard work. It's bloody hard work.

Pre-children, I had a glimpse into the life of a parent while I was working in a creative partnership with a new father called James.

I would leave my easy life of leisure outside work to come into the office and sit down with a resigned look that said, *Right, let's get down to this then*. James would come into the office and slump down into the chair with a look of total relief, as if this was his time of leisure. And in many senses, it was.

Yes, bloody hard work: I'll be at peace when they're off to school, for sure.

I'LL BE AT PEACE WHEN... WE MANAGE TO PAY THE BILLS AND MORTGAGE

Many people suffer from financial insecurity in one way or another, and most of it will entail a good degree of 'I'll be at peace when...'. And it can come down to whether we have enough money to pay the bills and mortgage or rent each month.

I have, in the past, exhibited a common pattern around money (I seem to have cured myself of it, but we'll see). I'd spend months not really knowing our financial situation in detail – just assuming it was kind of OK, and thus not worrying about it. And then I'd force myself (or be forced by some large tax bill) to look at everything properly; this would cause me lots of worry and pain, so I'd soon be back to burying my head in the sand.

I was supported in this pattern by the fiendishly complicated tax system here in Italy. It's practically impossible to understand how exactly we're taxed; *and* the rules change every year anyway; *and* taxes are rather high. This meant that, whatever happened, I could always blame the taxman and/or the accountant.

Anyway, now that I've kicked that habit, and know what's going on without freaking out, I have a more predictable curve in my state of mind around money and our business: when we're meeting or exceeding our forecasts I tend to feel OK, and if we're behind our forecasts, I'm more anxious.

And you could argue that this is fine, as that anxiety incentivizes me to find ways to improve our results as a business (so it's far better than the head-in-the-sand obliviousness to the early warning signs). But I can easily, therefore, lead a life of 'I'll be at peace when we meet our forecasts.'

In one way or another, many of us believe we'll be at peace when we're able to pay this or that, or when we've paid off this or that. But, generally speaking, the relief of paying off one thing is soon smothered by the anxiety arising from having to pay for something else.

I'LL BE AT PEACE WHEN... WE HAVE A LARGER HOUSE

We have laundry drying in the lounge all the time; the kids really should have their own rooms by now; I've had it with working at the kitchen table; the garden is tiny; all our friends have bigger houses; there's no room to swing a cat in here. The place was fine when we bought it, but now... If only we could afford a larger house, then everything would be tickety-boo.

I'LL BE AT PEACE WHEN... THE HOUSE IS TIDY

I was born with two opposing preferences that have doomed me to everlasting domestic misery:

* The desire for a tidy, organized space

* A dislike of tidying and organizing

My desire for a tidy and organized space, whether at home or in the office, isn't just a flippant desire – such as, *I'd like to drive a Ferrari round the Imola motorsport race circuit*. It's one that affects my every waking (and maybe sleeping) moment. I don't have to go into energetic/Feng Shui reasons to know that I simply feel better in a clear and tidy space; and I feel more uncomfortable in a messy space.

But I don't like tidying. And neither does Gaia. And we have teenage boys. You get the picture. So, yes, we have a cleaner. But once she's left, and we're all in the house – and especially if we're eating – it takes about half an hour for it all to go to (dirty) pot.

I've adopted strategies over the years to cope with this: to find my (slightly tidier) way through the mess. I currently fence off certain areas of my life that I then keep tidy and clear. So the area next to my side of the bed – a table and an Ikea bookshelf system containing my favourite books, family photos and precious personal items – is immaculately tidy and clean. I know that this area, at least, is tidy.

When our home is so untidy that I have to navigate an obstacle course to arrive at the bedroom, I'll stand looking at 'my corner' to calm myself down. Even then I sometimes have to 'blinker' my eyes so I can't see Gaia's side of the bedroom (think 1970s squat with Italian style).

The other fenced-off area is my car. I can't bear to sit in Gaia's car, as she simply doesn't understand why anyone would want to keep a nice clean car. This is Gaia's car: empty water bottles, receipts, biscuit wrappers, an apple core, coins, a banana skin, yoga mats and cushions, a box with miscellaneous items collected during a long-ago-attempted tidy, a screenwash bottle (leaking), a high-visibility jacket (unfolded, creased and dirty), a beach umbrella (all year round), a golf umbrella (borrowed from a hotel, but then kept). And this is not an exhaustive list.

I shudder and shake my head when I look into her car. She shudders and shakes her head when she sits in mine. She tries to relax by putting her foot up on my immaculate dashboard – so I reach across and tap her ankle.

No matter how much time Gaia spends in my car – and no matter what I say to her about taking her things with her, and reminding her that I've just had it cleaned – this is what I find in the passenger seat footwell when I next get in: an empty Tupperware container with a spoon in it and the remains of something oily and yoghurty; discarded tissues/kitchen paper; the inevitable water bottle with a quarter of the water remaining; and that dusty footprint on the dashboard.

If I ever say anything about this, Gaia just shakes her head, appalled at my bourgeois insistence on orderliness. But still, once it's been cleaned up after a Gaia visit, my car is my refuge. Without driving a metre, I'm transported to calmness and tranquillity. And I'm guessing that if our house were anything like my car, yes goddammit, I would be at peace.

I'LL BE AT PEACE WHEN...
I'M A SUCCESS

Have you enjoyed success in your life? Most of us have, in one thing or another. And I think all of us should. However, it clearly depends on how you define 'success'. If your definition of success is very narrow and consists only of 'winning a Nobel Prize', then your experience of life will be very different from that of someone who enjoys all the successes they have along the way. From getting a gold star in nursery to attaining good exam results; from achieving something great in a sport, to getting their first job... and so on.

I've enjoyed successes, large and small, in my life; just as I've endured failures, large and small. I make a to-do list every day and I enjoy the 'success' of ticking each thing off. Those small daily successes often lead to bigger successes in my life (so today's list includes writing three sections of this book; a future success would be lots of people reading the chapters of this book; and a greater success still would be lots of people feeling more 'at peace' in their lives because of it).

But here's what I've found with success on any scale: although we use the word 'enjoy' around it, that enjoyment doesn't last long. When I hear about any success of mine or ours, I enjoy it for a few moments, and then I quickly move on to the next thing to achieve. I'm not good at enjoying success, and simply being at peace with having achieved something great; this is probably because, underneath, I believe that 'being at peace' is not conducive to achieving success, and that success comes from a perpetual restlessness.

I wish you success, if only so you'll see that it's not the ultimate answer; I also hope that you may 'enjoy' that success for longer.

LEVEL 1 HACK

Hang out with someone who doesn't see life in this Level 1 way – constantly looking to the next thing to get through so they can be happy. There are a few around. They're usually not meditation or yoga teachers. They probably work in the corner shop.

I'LL BE AT PEACE WHEN... I'M WEALTHY

In this world, some successes can lead to wealth. And like success, our definition of wealth can vary hugely.

What does 'wealth' mean to you? Of course, if you sat down and compared your lifestyle and prosperity with that of the least fortunate people on the planet, you'd likely feel very wealthy. But most people see wealth as somewhere else. Even relatively wealthy people are likely to see real wealth elsewhere – in others' salaries, second homes and stock portfolios. Most people, in other words, would like more.

A survey asked a group of very wealthy people – from millionaires to billionaires – if they felt content with their level of wealth. Most said 'no'. They were then asked, 'How much more would make you feel content?' And they were invited to put a $ figure on it. The researchers turned that figure into the percentage of extra wealth that the wealthy people wanted in order to feel content. The figure was, roughly, the same for all of them: 20% extra.

It seems then, that everyone is 20% away from being content, regardless of their income. And that's worth bearing in mind as you go about wanting more wealth, more things, and trying to get them. If you believe that you'll be at peace when you're wealthy, the research suggests you'll remain forever 20% away from peace.

I'LL BE AT PEACE WHEN... I WIN THAT AWARD

Even if we're doing a job we like, or have achieved what we regard as success, there's usually something else that we're hankering after. It might be an award or an accolade of some sort; it might be an honorary position. But there's usually something that keeps us motivated to keep at it – to achieve more, to hit greater heights, to stand out for what we do, to make a mark, to create a legacy.

And that's a good thing, isn't it? If the incentives are incentivizing enough, everyone benefits from the common pursuit of excellence. More people achieve excellence and we all then benefit from these various excellences: whether it's in science or engineering or medicine or the arts, or whatever you'd regard as most beneficial to your existence.

The thing is, those chasing the award or accolade are not at peace until it's won. In fact, many regard 'not being at peace' as a positive thing. Sure, we dress it in other language – like 'drive', 'determination', 'ambition' – but it amounts to the same thing. We've persuaded ourselves that a certain kind of restlessness is critical for our common progress.

I'LL BE AT PEACE WHEN... I'VE LOST THIS WEIGHT

Bummer, I just got up to make myself a few slices of brown bread and butter, only to sit down again and see this subject heading on my list.

I spend a good amount of time pondering how to lose weight. I contemplate what meals to eat and which foods to avoid; I decide whether to fast or just skip one meal; whether to go on that proper diet that really worked for me last time, or just try to eat naturally without obsessing about it. I exceed my 10,000 steps each day, but it's not that many calories really (in fact, I think I've eaten those calories in the buttered bread and the accompanying watermelon slices I've just eaten).

I'm certainly not at peace when I'm thinking about food and my weight. And I assume I'd be more at peace if I could lose this weight: I'd be more comfortable in my own (less padded) skin, happier when catching my reflection in a shop window, and more at ease on the beach (though I do sometimes wonder if I'm not quite uncomfortable enough with my belly, and thus not sufficiently motivated to lose it).

The problem with weight issues is that we face a unique self-sabotaging opposition when trying to deal with them. It goes something like this: we begin by not feeling good (our weight problems often contribute to this), and know that we'd probably feel better if we could lose the weight. But our more natural response to not feeling good is to eat. But eating takes us further away from losing weight. And we feel worse.

So, what's the answer here? First, within the theme of this part of the book, it's to be aware that it's unlikely – even if we do lose the weight – we'll be fully at peace, and all our problems will end. Second, it's to recognize that the improvement in mood we feel when we eat (and then overeat) is usually temporary and a way of numbing the emotions.

So, whether it's the side of us that thinks eating is the answer to being at peace (i.e. in the short term) or the side that thinks not eating (so much) is the answer to being at peace, both are probably wrong. We need to find our peace elsewhere. And in doing so, our weight issues might well resolve naturally. This is what many people have found out for themselves. Lucky beggars.

I'LL BE AT PEACE WHEN...
I'M WELL AGAIN

This one, I really know. When I was aged three or so, I ate some tuna – something I'd happily eaten before – and had an allergic reaction to it. I went on to develop (not intentionally) allergies to a whole variety of things, and the allergic response manifested itself in a variety of symptoms. Since that time, I've experienced long periods of chronic illness and short, spectacular acute emergencies.

So I'm familiar with both chronic and acute illness. And they both have the same effect on my head in that I believe I could be at peace if only I could get better. Well, that's how I've responded as an adult. I do know that, as an at times very sick child, I didn't much contemplate my illness, or the possibility of getting better (or not). I was sick and that was that – I didn't think 'that's that', of course.

But when I entered a long period of chronic illness as a young adult, I longed to be well. My symptoms would vary, but were generally very uncomfortable and sometimes simply embarrassing. I imagined that, if only I could be well, then I'd have nothing else to worry about. My health was my main worry, and everything else seemed kind of trivial in comparison.

I couldn't understand why people without such debilitating symptoms were worrying so much. 'What do they have to worry about? They don't realize how lucky they are' was a favourite mantra of mine. I dreamed about what it would be like to be 'normal' (this is how I naively saw the rest of the non-suffering world), and not have to suffer as I did.

But I got to find out what it's like to be 'normal', as I saw it. Because, since 2005 (and a period of healing I connect with 'F**k It' – as described in the book *F**k It, the Ultimate Spiritual Way*), I've been largely free of symptoms. I'm still allergic to stuff: I can't eat fish or nuts or share a small room with a dog; and I don't have any issue with that. When people hear that I can't eat fish, they often say, 'Oohh, that must be terrible.' My response is: 'No, it's not – what *is* terrible is the symptoms I'd get if I ate the fish.'

So, what's it like, being normal? I think you know the answer. Having suffered for so long, I did spend a good amount of time really appreciating being well. I lived happily in the comparison with how I'd been. I enjoyed eating normally, drinking normally and living normally.

But, rather sooner than I expected, other worries and concerns emerged, like weeds, in my head. And most of them had less obvious solutions (than 'getting better').

And that was with the chronic illness. The acute side presents a more intense manifestation of this same phenomenon, though. Every two or three years, I eat something by mistake that contains an allergen that has the potential to kill me. I've not had a serious anaphylactic shock for 25 years. When I did have one, the reaction (to nuts in a Danish pastry) took five hours to reach its life-threatening crescendo.

So when I eat something I shouldn't (in an allergen sense, not a cream cake sense), I tend to experience the same early-stage symptoms: it's just difficult to predict which way it will go – whether the symptoms will slowly diminish, or whether they'll worsen.

Therefore, I tend to get myself close to a hospital emergency room (I don't enter it, as they'd hit me with various drugs) and sit it out. When the symptoms are intensifying (it takes a while for the crippling stomach cramps to kick in), I get seriously worried, and I try to calm myself down.

I have the same conversation with myself every time. It goes something like this: *This is serious. Bloody hell. Why have you been worrying about such stupid things recently? Jeez, they don't matter. Why do you never understand that? Just be happy to be alive. Be happy to be well. Be happy to be with what you've got.*

And I reply (to myself): *I know, I know. You're right. But if we get through this one, I'll change. I'll relax more. I'll keep things in perspective. You're right – we just need to be happy to be alive. It's good to be reminded.*

Yes, but we've been reminded before. Why do you never remember? And so on.

The symptoms then diminish, and I breathe a sigh of relief. I spend the rest of the day appreciating life like a man let out of prison. I go to bed, just happy to be alive. Nothing more needed. I wake up the next morning, and the worries rush back in.

Don't get me wrong, I love being well (when I am – as I am now), but I'm the expert in knowing that 'getting better' is just another place where the peace thing keeps running ahead of you. And that's the feeling, isn't it? We catch up with it for a moment. We get the job, the boy/girl, the healing, the award; or we go on holiday or get some great news… and we're at peace. But then off it runs again. And off we go, chasing after it.

LEVEL 1 HACK

Turn to Level 2 – you've got this, haven't you?

I'LL BE AT PEACE WHEN... I CAN TAKE REDUNDANCY

The timing is perfect. I've not been happy here recently: it's not what I expected, and there's not much opportunity for promotion. I could do with a rest too – maybe rethink things, or do some travelling. It's been a long time.

And I now hear that they're looking to make some redundancies (layoffs), and that they're likely to offer voluntary redundancies first. That would be perfect – just perfect. It means I could take time out, and maybe make a new start. Crikey, yes: I really want this.

The thing is, I've spent all these years trying to show how indispensable I am. I now have to demonstrate that they can do without me, but

57

that I'm not too keen to go. (Or maybe they'll assume I'll go anyway, without being paid. Blimey, I really want this.)

I really do feel that I'll be at peace when I can take redundancy.

I'LL BE AT PEACE WHEN... THE HOLIDAYS ARRIVE

In the stress, rush and madness of everyday life, we all like to have a booked future holiday glowing in our diaries. We usually see the benefits of a holiday in terms of the pleasure and rest we get while we're away, and then how we bring our refreshed selves back into normal life.

But the benefits of a holiday begin the moment we plan it. When it's all feeling too much, we remember that we have our holiday booked. When we're exhausted and stressed, we think of our holiday. When it's dark, grey and raining, we think of the holiday. Whatever we're feeling, we know we'll be at peace when the holidays arrive.

And many of us are fortunate enough to have been able to craft the kind of holiday that hits the spot for us, 'at peace' wise. If there's one area of our lives in which we consciously try to create the perfect environment for feeling at peace, it's the holidays. In the annual schedule of our lives, we leave two weeks (or whatever) free to paint our idea of life perfection.

So what's your ideal holiday haven/heaven? Though we live in Italy (close to the sea), the Italian beach is still our favourite family holiday destination (in another part of Italy, Sicily). We like huddling in the shade of our beach umbrella on a wild(ish) sandy beach; picnicking on ciabatta with Pecorino cheese and sun-dried tomatoes; snorkelling in the clear, warm sea; wandering around fishing villages at night, and sleeping under a fan. As our boys hit 16 (in 3 days' time), it's special just to be together for a couple of weeks. And we leave for Sicily in seven days.

You have to hand it to us humans for this system we've created for living: by dropping refreshing holidays in at regular intervals, we can tolerate a lot more in our everyday lives. The holiday environment, too, reminds us that, no matter how terrible we're feeling back at home (and work), there'll always exist a place like this where we can feel at peace.

Because the truth is that we do feel at peace on holiday, don't we? The dramatic change in geography, climate, routine, cuisine, language – and the fact that our diaries have been cleared of all the usual commitments, responsibilities and stresses – leads us to feel at peace.

And the knowledge that there's an actual place on the planet where we could feel at peace, in comparison to what we feel now, is reassuring. The thing is, that could be the problem, couldn't it? If we didn't have this idealized 'at peace' experience dangling tantalizingly and reassuringly over every other moment of our more humdrum existence, maybe we'd be more able to find peace in the present.

I'LL BE AT PEACE WHEN... WE HAVE A CHANGE OF GOVERNMENT

I see so much injustice everywhere. This government has squeezed the poor and needy for every last penny; it's run down the health service; and then it helps the rich get richer. They're only looking after their own: their friends in the City, and their private school chums. There's no one looking out for ordinary working people anymore.

Our children can hardly afford to rent somewhere to live, never mind buy a house. Jobs are not secure anymore. The term 'zero-hours contracts' says it all – how can any contract be zero-hours? Might as well call them zero-money contracts.

This government might say it's there for the working people, but it's a lie. There's only hardship and misery. How can we possibly be at peace when we have a government like this?

I'LL BE AT PEACE WHEN... I'VE PAID OFF THE MORTGAGE

A mortgage is a 25-year peace-delayer. Even with historically low interest rates, your mortgage, if you have one, is likely to be your most significant outgoing. Financially, then, it's the main reason you work. And thus the main reason you *have* to work.

Justifiably or not, many people see the paying off of the mortgage as a herald of a new era of freedom. Even though the home accounts might not back this up (i.e. there are other costs to living), there's a sense that the heavy ties of obligation to our job loosen somewhat when the monthly mortgage payments end.

And so, 'when I've paid off the mortgage' becomes another significant asset in our personal bank of 'I'll be at peace when...'s.

I'LL BE AT PEACE WHEN... THE DIVORCE IS SETTLED

Everyone says that divorce is one of the most stressful experiences in life; and I'm finding this so difficult. I just want to get it over with now. I wish it didn't take so long. This is unbearable, and the effect it's having on the kids is breaking my heart.

At least when it's over, we can all just settle and know where we are, and be at peace.

LEVEL 1 HACK

Don't wish this on yourself – it's an inadvertent hack – but when shit happens big time, you'll be hit by perspective, and the realization that you have to live more in the moment.

I'LL BE AT PEACE WHEN... I / WE RETIRE

They've just raised the retirement age again; it seems like every couple of years they raise it by a couple of years. Are they raising it at the same rate that we're living? Will retirement forever remain 10 or 20 or 30 (however old you are) years ahead of you?

People see retirement in different ways: some look forward to it, while others dread it; some never even think about it. But many of us still see the prospect of retirement as one long holiday. Which I suppose, if you retire to a warm foreign clime or you're wealthy enough for regular trips there, it can be.

Or seem to be, from this side of retirement. Because, even though there'll be similarities with what pre-retirees see as a 'holiday' – i.e.

the sun, the sangria and long lazy days – there will be differences too. Because our pre-retirement concept of a 'holiday' is protected by its short-burst nature.

The holiday environment is so attractive because it's so different to what we're used to. And we don't get long enough to get used to it. We're back in the normal way of life before we know it, keeping 'holiday' preserved as a special oasis for our hopes and dreams.

But stay on the beach and drink the sangria for longer than a couple of months, and your concept of this perfect holiday destination begins to change. When you start to complain about things at the resort, and find people annoying, and worry about things, and get bored, you might at first think it's the *place* that doesn't really suit you, after all. But, of course, it's the fact that we take ourselves with us wherever we go. And though the moany, worrying side might be quiet for a couple of weeks a year, it will want to have its say, sooner or later.

So, even if your retirement looks from the outside like one long holiday, it's unlikely to be the notion of 'holiday' you're used to. And, however it looks, retirement will reveal the same truths that everything else in our lives reveals – it's probably not the answer or the destination.

The problem with the idea of 'retirement', as opposed to, say, getting your own home, is that you can get stuck with its peace-dangling delusion for decades.

I'LL BE AT PEACE WHEN...
THE OPERATION IS OVER

I can imagine a hundred things that could disturb the anticipated peace of retirement, and one of them must be medical intervention.

There's a unique combination of discomfort in the period before a serious medical intervention: the discomfort created by whatever it is that it's necessary to intervene in (some type of pain or incapacity) and the discomfort of the anticipation of the medical intervention itself (which clearly depends on our level of anxiety around such things).

It must, therefore, be rather difficult, with this double whammy of discomfort, to feel fully at peace in a pre-op environment.

I'LL BE AT PEACE WHEN... THIS PAIN HAS GONE

Pain is hard to deal with, and it's certainly hard to be at peace with it. In fact, that's one of the points of pain: it's the body's way of saying to you, 'Oi, you, there's something wrong here: can you do something about it please? Don't just sit around feeling all "at peace".'

Pain is another of the body's self-regulation mechanisms – a red light flashing on the dashboard of our nervous system. Disturbing us from our peace, in order to make us act and sort out the problem, is good programming. The difficulty is with chronic pain, which can't easily be relieved

The idea that we'll only find peace when the pain has gone is flawed, for two reasons. The final 'peace' we feel is likely to be short-lived, as we've found again and again in this Level 1 section of the book, and thus not worth the expectation we have of it. And that idea – that 'peace will come when...' – does, as usual, prevent us from searching for ways to find peace now.

Now, you may see that it's probably easier for someone who believes they'll find peace when they get that big promotion to recognize this delusion – and attempt to find peace in the present – than it is for someone in great pain to see it. And that's what makes pain such a great teacher. And maybe why, generally speaking, the pain-loading in our lives tends to be weighted more towards the final years, as we wear out.

Whatever peace we can find in the midst of pain is a hard-won and highly valuable peace (not that peace has a value scale, but I'm sure you see my point).

LEVEL 1 HACK

Work hard, dream big… get through as many of these as quickly as you can – except the death thing – so you repeatedly get the message that there's always another thing. You'll thus hasten your way to Level 2.

I'LL BE AT PEACE WHEN... I'M RESTING IN PEACE

'Rest in peace', we say, and hope for, when someone dies. No one knows what, if anything, awaits us on the other side, but as death brings the simple cessation of what the majority of human beings experience while alive – i.e. they're neither resting nor being at peace – it's probably sufficiently close to 'rest' and 'peace' for most.

And many people do, at some point in their lives, believe that the only way to be at peace is to be no more. These can be the dark thoughts of the desperate, or of those who are considering taking their own lives, or a readiness in the elderly to 'go' (which is something you might have seen in your own relatives).

But I've placed the peace that death brings in Level 1 intentionally. The 'I'll be at peace when...' precept is a delusion. We've seen that, at best, the peace and happiness gained is woefully short-lived. And maybe it's the same with death. The dying of the light which then (possibly) finales with a growing of the light and a sense of peace is then (literally) short-lived, as consciousness is (most likely) snuffed out.

Because the kind of 'peace' that most of us are after is one that we can be conscious of. And the truth is, as we've seen, it's a fool's game to believe we can find that peace by chasing after it. It's a mouse wheel that never stops turning. The only logical answer is to see that it's possible to stop running – to let the wheel slow down – and find peace in the present.

LEVEL 2

I CAN BE AT PEACE NOW

Diary entry: 7 August 2017 – Honking the Horn of Peace

We're on holiday. We're sitting on the balcony of our villa (on the west coast of Sicily), looking out over the sea.

Below, on the narrow road between our villa and the beach, comes the honking sound of a car horn and voices. I look down and see a rubbish lorry (i.e. a lorry that collects rubbish, not an inferior lorry), crawling along at walking pace as a rubbish man (a man who collects the rubbish, not an inferior man) picks up the rubbish bags (you get the picture) from outside the houses and throws them into the back of the lorry.

Behind the lorry is a small car with a couple inside. They're driving one metre behind the back of the (smelly) lorry, and are clearly frustrated. But they can't get past because there are cars parked on both sides of this narrow road, and there's no room for the lorry to pull over (even if it wanted to).

It's unlikely that the couple in the car have anywhere urgent to be. They're probably just going to the beach, as that's all there is… beach. I would bet they're from the city, most likely Milan. They believe that peace and happiness lie on the other side of the lorry, on the beach. But this lorry isn't going to be moving over for a while.

Result: stress. A horn-honking-tapping-the-steering-wheel-cursing-these-rubbish-people (i.e. people inferior to them) stress. And that, as we've seen, is how most of us live our lives. The answer for the couple in the car – given the absolute, unchangeable reality of the slow-driving lorry – is to sit back and relax, and find some peace before the moment they hit the beach.

The answer for them, and for us, is to find some peace now.

Yes, it's time for Level 2.

We take a big step forward in life when we recognize that working out what we'd like to feel is more important than working out what we'd like to do, or whatever other aim we have in life. And if we realize that feeling 'at peace' is one of the highest aims in itself, then Level 1 is indeed a high starting level. Like the opening rounds of the World Cup Final in football, you have to be a top team and a top player to get there in the first place.

The beautiful further realization that if being at peace is your aim, then maybe you can feel at peace *now*, is powerful and potentially life-changing. If being a stone (14lbs) lighter is your aim, then it's clearly impossible to be a stone lighter *now*. If having a larger house is your aim, then that's equally difficult to have *now*. But we do have the potential to be at peace now.

You could argue that, if you're lost on the plains of Africa and a lion is running towards you, then feeling at peace now is as difficult as being a stone lighter. And yet the high number of people who report experiencing a sense of peace in such extremely stressful, life-threatening situations indicates that it's not impossible to do so, but possibly even likely.

So it does seem that we have as much ability to feel a sense of peace now as we do the ability to clench our fists. We just don't realize that we do.

And clenching a fist was something I did as part of the first relaxation exercises I learned, back in 1990. I'd realized that stress and tension were a problem for me and my health, so I'd bought some relaxation tapes (a pre-streaming analogue audio delivery system). More detail on the clenching-fist technique later...

LEVEL 2 HACK

Giggle at those who take 'peace' very
seriously. Giggle at the mindfulness
addicts, the crossed-legged yogis,
the shaven-headed mini-Buddhas,
the peace brigade, the vegan
proselytizers, and the levitating Reiki
rabble. And giggle at yourself as the
peace drops on you and you start
to feel blissed out, holy and woken.

I CAN RELAX NOW

Ever since I listened to those tapes in 1990, I've been teaching people how to relax. So, while teaching a Qigong (the Chinese healing art) retreat on the volcanic island of Stromboli in Sicily last month, I intended to talk about relaxation, and how to relax in just about any circumstances.

I asked the group for a show of hands in response to the following question (you can answer it, too): 'Who knows how to relax *now*, without the help of whatever you normally use to relax – whether it's calming music, a yoga stretch or a glass of wine?'

Usually only three or four people (out of a group of 20) raise their hands. And it's often the case that they've been on a retreat with me before (so I should hope they'd know). I then usually go about teaching them various techniques (which I'll teach you), until more and more people are able to put up their hand (slowly, and in a very relaxed manner).

Even after a few more days of being on holiday and learning the best relaxation techniques money can buy, there are usually a couple of people who still don't feel they can raise their hand in response to this question – so I just drop a Valium into their Aperol Spritz before dinner.

On this particular afternoon, after asking the question and getting the usual small show of hands, I tried something different. Rather than launching into my usual talk about how relaxation works, and how to relax, I asked the group to walk around the rooftop terrace of the retreat at a regular pace. Then I said to them: 'Just relax, now.' Many of them slowed down, and I could feel the relaxation just happen.

'Good,' I continued, 'now you know what it's like to relax: you just… relax.'

Then I asked the participants to return to their previous state, and they all started walking more quickly; then I asked them to relax again. I did this a few times so that they got used to this movement – from tense to relaxed and back again – and also so that they'd start to notice the difference between the states.

And you can do this now: it really does save a lot of time and effort learning elaborate relaxation exercises:

* Just… relax.

* Then go back to not being so relaxed.

* And then relax again.

* Notice the difference between the two states.

When I asked the group, again, after 10 minutes: 'Who knows how to relax *now*, without the help of whatever you normally use to relax – whether it's calming music, a yoga stretch or a glass of wine?', most people put up their hand.

It was the quickest, most successful relaxation masterclass I'd led in 30 years. It was from the Nike school of peace training: Just Relax. And for those who didn't put up their hand? I dropped a couple of tabs of Valium into my bag for later.

LEVEL 2 FACT

Over time, meditation appears to shrink the 'amygdala', the 'fight or flight' area of the brain, and thicken the pre-frontal cortex, the area of the brain related to higher order functions such as decision-making and awareness.[1]

---

1 Source: *Scientific American* magazine

HOW PEACEFUL
AM I NOW?

In talking about being 'relaxed', I've assumed that a sense of peace accompanies relaxation. It does for me: to feel more at peace, I just need to relax more. But it might be different for you. It's time to find out.

To be more at peace now, we need to know how at peace, or not, we actually are. For an air-conditioning system to work, and either cool or warm the air accordingly, the system first needs to know the current ambient temperature. So the thermostat is essential to any heating/cooling system.

When it comes to knowing how they are, most people don't have much of a thermostat. They don't really know how they're feeling. They're not aware of their relative levels of tension and relaxation;

they don't know whether they feel particularly happy or sad – they don't think about it.

This may surprise you. If you're hyper-aware of how you're feeling, it may seem impossible that a person can be oblivious of his or her feelings. But we've seen over the years, in our retreat groups, that there are always those who simply don't know how they feel, and who have great difficulty contacting any feelings.

Why is this? Well it's likely that they've had to switch off their thermostat. If our thermostat constantly reads a temperature that we don't like, then maybe it's best to switch it off and not know.

I can relate to that literally – and it's probably the reason I chose 'air conditioning' as the analogy just now – as it's so hot where we are at the moment (it was 42°C/107°F on our car thermostat at midday today), that I'd kind of prefer not to know the temperature.

Knowing it's so hot makes it feel even hotter. The other day I read an article about the likely effect of rising temperatures and humidity levels in certain parts of the world in years to come: in short… death. Apparently, if the combination of temperature and humidity reach a high enough level, then our bodies will not be able to sweat sufficiently to reduce our temperature. And we'll die. The article said that we humans would not be able to last more than six hours in such conditions, even if we stayed in the shade.

I'd not imagined this possibility in such a vivid way before. And now I can't forget it. Like certain things you see in life that you'd love to forget, but can't. And what comes to mind now is something that happened when I was around eight years old.

It was a Sunday and my parents had family friends round for lunch; let's call them the Smiths. After we'd eaten, I needed to go to the loo, for a number one, and went to the downstairs toilet. I opened the door, and there was Mrs Smith – sitting there with her tights and knickers around her ankles. Nooooooo.

It was a sight I'll never forget. Maybe in my dying moments on this planet, I won't see a tunnel of white light and feel a sense of immense enveloping peace, but see Mrs Smith sitting there having a poo; and my last enveloping sense will be Noooooo.

LEVEL 2 HACK

Mix your increasing experience of peace with an equal and opposite exposure to the noise and distraction of life. Find the noise, the mess, the escapist film or book or Facebook page and lose yourself in it.

So, how do you tune up your thermostat? Back in 1990, the relaxation exercise I learned involved tensing up different parts of the body, then relaxing them. The first thing I'd do was clench my fists, then release them. You can do that now: simply make a fist – really clench that fist – and notice what it feels like. Then relax your hand, and notice what that feels like. You can go around your whole body doing the same thing.

In doing so, you're training yourself to identify the two extreme states that likely exist either side of where you normally exist. So, now, maybe you're naturally slightly tense about something in the background, but generally quite relaxed as you read these words. You're not really tense, like the clenched fist. And you're probably not really relaxed either, like the relaxed and limp unclenched fist.

So feeling these two surrounding states begins to tune our 'state' thermostat. We're tuning it to recognize a high temperature (the highly tense state) and a low temperature (the deeply relaxed state).

By reading these extremes, you'll now start to get a sense of a scale between them too. And this will develop as you start to use your thermostat. And to do that, you simply need to ask yourself, *How am I feeling?* At the moment we're looking at how tense/at peace you are, but there's clearly a huge spectrum of potential responses here.

So if I ask myself now, *How am I feeling?* (on the tense/at peace scale), the answer would be *somewhere just below midway*. I'm not stressed, but neither am I fully relaxed and at peace. There's a lot going on around me, including persistent requests from a four-year-old girl to help her colour in her fairy castle.

If I ask *How am I feeling?* more widely, I get this: *a little tired, a little full, a little spacey, a little uncomfortable about something I can't quite put my finger on, and a little restless.* Nothing is strong and full-on: hence the 'little's.

And – before you go away and practise this – you can add another element to it: don't judge what you notice too strongly (and preferably not at all). There will be times of course when you need to act on what you notice. If you notice you're feeling really tired, for example, then have a rest and go to bed earlier if you can. In the same way that, if my car thermostat reads 42°C/107°F, I'm probably better off staying in the air-conditioned interior than venturing into the desert-like external world of Sicily.

But, generally speaking, try to notice without engaging too much, and without judging too harshly. This is important. Remember: the reason many of us have disabled our thermostats is that we haven't liked what they were reading.

The ability to subdue some of this like/dislike response to the thermostat readings is critical to our desire to keep the thermostat on and working. If I ask myself *How am I feeling?* and the answer is, *Sad and upset, and so tired of this pain in my hip,* I'll tend to engage strongly with this response, and get caught up in a negative thought process: *Why am I so sad and upset again? Why can't I just be happy? I've nothing to complain about, after all. And this pain in my hip is probably something serious, maybe arthritis. Maybe I'll have to have a hip replacement,* and so on.

So, how can we engage less with what we notice? An effective way to practise this is to add the words 'that's interesting' to whatever it is we're noticing. It's a neutral, acknowledging response, but it stops the over-engagement that our mind tends towards. Try it out:

I'm sad and upset... that's interesting; I'm tired of this pain in my hip... that's interesting. That kind of thing. You might occasionally want to punch the 'that's interesting' voice in the mouth until it can no longer speak... *well, that's interesting.*

We are, then, aiming to notice more (engaging the thermostat) while judging less. This process, in itself, is likely to increase your levels of peace (and as we'll see later, it's akin to aspects of meditation). But the primary reason is to sensitize yourself more to how you are, so that you work more effectively with where you'd like to be.

It's when you observe that you're not at peace, now, that you engage your ability to find peace, now. This process may seem somewhat clunky at the beginning, but it becomes more and more natural, until you have a persistent sense of how you are and how you're feeling, and then adjust accordingly.

There are, of course, many other ways to measure how you are, state-wise. If you find yourself moaning and complaining a lot, you're probably quite low on the 'at peace' scale. Likewise, if you find it difficult to sit still.

A great indicator for me at the moment is the presence of small humans. We're on holiday with friends who have a four-year-old girl (they gave birth to her, it's not just that they happen to 'have' her): the one who wants help with her colouring-in. Now, if I'm relaxed and peaceful, she wants to be with me. If I'm not, she doesn't. She's my thermostat.

Pets, I've found, can be the same. Well, I only know what it's like with cats – because we've had cats – but not dogs, or rabbits, or guinea pigs, or snakes. With cats (and possibly the rest of the list too), we soon learn that they respond to us more when we're relaxed, so we relax to be with them, and then being with them relaxes us more.

And this is the idea behind any kind of thermostat we use: we see the current temperature and that allows us to adjust the temperature rapidly to the desired level. So let's look at more ways to rapidly adjust the temperature.

LEVEL 2 HACK

As soon as you can in your practice,
enjoy feeling superior to stressed-out
non-peace-seekers. It's going to
happen at some point, so you might
as well get it out of the way now. Do
enjoy it though. It's like seeing other
fatsos when you're on a diet. They
may be no heavier than you, but unlike
you, they're not on the enlightened
path to leanness. Heathens.

I CAN BE GRATEFUL NOW

Being grateful for stuff might be your natural disposition, but for most people, it isn't. Most of us focus on what's wrong, and what we don't have, rather than on what's right and what we do have.

You could argue that such a focus motivates us towards constant improvement, both personally and in society as a whole. It's this focus that drives us on and drives up our country's GDP figures each year. Where would the economy (and the advertising industry) be if people were happy with what they have, rather than always striving for more? Yet being grateful for what we have is a powerful way to access peace in our lives.

It's a good idea, then, to spend more time every day being grateful for what you have. People call this 'gratitude practice', but that's like calling sitting quietly 'meditation': it over-formalizes and separates something that can just be a natural part of our lives. When I'm feeling out of sorts, or find myself moaning about things, I tend to list what I'm grateful for – like this:

I'm grateful for this sunshine and the blue sky; I'm grateful for my (generally) functioning body and the ability to walk; I'm grateful for Gaia and the boys; I'm grateful for all that we have – the things that make our lives more comfortable and the cars to take us to new, exciting places; I'm grateful for our business and all the people who attend our retreats and courses and buy our books (that's you); I'm grateful for another day alive on this beautiful and crazy planet.

I realized the other day that I use gratefulness as a primary tool when meeting challenges. We'd just arrived at our holiday destination: a four-bedroom villa on the west coast of Sicily. It had seemed OK when we booked it: although it was relatively cheap, it looked comfortable, was located right on the seafront, and had good reviews.

The reality, however, was rather depressing (we had to go back to the website and look again at the photos). The villa had one good bedroom and three box rooms, including one without a window; the bathrooms were covered in mould; there was nowhere to park outside; the beach (shingly rather than sandy – and somewhat inferior to the beach in front of our own home) was packed with people and very average. Oh, and there was no air conditioning: it was 42°C/107°F when we arrived.

We adults were disappointed, to put it mildly. And as the depression took hold, I started to list what I was grateful for, and counted our blessings:

Well, we're on holiday together at least; and, with the boys now 16, there probably won't be that many more holidays like this with them. We can hear the sea crashing onto the beach from the villa, and I'll be able to hear that tonight, in bed, and that's a rare and beautiful experience.

I'm sure there'll be some fantastic beaches a short drive away... which there are, as I'm lying on one of them now: it's one of the most stupendous beaches I've ever been on, and deserted on an August bank holiday. *And the food will undoubtedly be fantastic, wherever we go...* which it is... and so on.

In that challenging moment (and I know it wasn't challenging in the grand scheme of things), when things were looking pretty gloomy for our annual summer holiday together, taking my attention off what was wrong and what we didn't have (like air conditioning) and focusing on what was right and what we did have, cheered me, settled me and allowed me to be at peace with us, our holiday, and the shitty half-built villa.

Being grateful, then, for who we are, what we do, what we have and our lives as they are, is a quick way to find peace in the now.

(You may well be wondering this: *Man, you shouldn't have been so easily accepting of the shitty situation. You should have tried to change to another villa, or complained about the state of the place: done SOMETHING about it at least.* And of course we contemplated alternatives – there weren't any – and then took what action we could: like asking for the bathrooms to be cleaned. But the basics of the place and the situation remained the same.)

The funny thing is that now, a few days later, we all feel rather good about the villa and its position. The beach is usually empty, and has plenty of space to park every day (we'd arrived on a busy weekend), and the sea is actually rather lovely to swim in first thing in the morning. The fans in the rooms just about do it at night (and feel more natural than harsh air conditioning). And we don't really notice the ugly aspects of the accommodation anymore.

I'm grateful that I've been able to share these insights with you. I'm grateful that you're there, reading these words, exploring this whole 'at peace' subject together. I'm grateful for this moment, as it is, now. And I'm grateful for the moment in which you're reading this – however much or little distance in time there is between these two moments.

I CAN SWITCH OFF
MY PHONE NOW

I love everyday realizations: those moments when we understand somewhat obvious things that we know can make a big difference in our lives.

It was on the F**k It Qigong retreat on Stromboli this summer that I had one of these prosaic epiphanies. I was greatly enjoying the space we were finding in the group sessions; I was easing people into the space gently. I'll tell you precisely how soon, but we'd do 10 minutes at a time just sitting around doing nothing. I was finding real peace in those periods, and that peace was spreading out into the rest of the day too.

I was curious, for myself, as to why I'm not able to find more time in my everyday life just to hang out like that. I concluded, as I normally do, that I'm just very busy: that I'm up early making breakfast for the family, and then, aside from 20 minutes' Qigong practice, it's pretty much all go for the rest of the day. I then made a promise to myself that I'd find more slots to just sit and be during the day and evening.

But, soon after waking one morning during that retreat, I had an everyday epiphany that revealed a truth I'd been deluding myself about for a long time. After getting up and having a pee, I grabbed my phone, and went outside onto the terrace. From there, it's possible to see out to sea – to the tiny island, more a rocky outcrop, of Strombilicchio, and, in the other direction, up towards the top of the volcano (which explodes every 20 minutes or so, sounding precisely like a thunderclap).

I sat down and looked at the view for a nanosecond before picking up my phone and starting to check out the news headlines. Then I realized something: this is what I do to cover the 'spaces' in my life. It's so obvious, but I hadn't spotted it before. I'd somehow discounted those little 'gaps' in the day when I'd normally just turn to my phone, as you probably do: the times when we're waiting for a bus or taxi, or we're early for a meeting, or we're eating a sandwich, and so on.

There are so many of these gaps and moments during the day that if we could just disable our phones, and not replace them with some other mode of distraction, we'd have the perfect practice opportunities for significantly increasing the levels of peace in our lives. So why don't we do that?

Well, I had a look at why *I* don't – at why I turn to my phone, like most of us do, at the slightest whiff of a gap in my daily life. I have no excuse, by the way, in 'utility': I'm not reading urgent emails or posting important promotions on Facebook; I'm usually just checking up on what Donald J. Trump has said or done that day.

I realize that I'm kind of scared (and not just by what Trump has said or done). I'm scared of the space, the gap (so it's funny that I fill it with fear-inducing stimulus). Yes, even me: I do this stuff for a living and have meditated, in one form or another, since I was 20 years old, yet facing the gap can bother me.

If I enter the gap, I have to face my own thoughts and feelings. I – along with close to 7 billion others – have to face any worries or fears or guilt or longing or discontent. So many of us long to be at peace, to be calmer, and have more space in our hectic lives… yet what we do with these little offerings of space reveals to us that the real picture is more complicated.

No matter how much you say you'd like to be at peace; no matter how much you realize that the putting-off-peace game of Level 1 is a fool's game, and that you could actually feel peace in the now; no matter how much you convince yourself that there's not enough time to be at peace. The most powerful app on your phone is the reminder it gives you, each time you look at it, that you're unable to just be still – to sit without distraction.

Just to sit still. And be.

Which is what I'm going to do now – before I guide you through how to face those fears and just sit there yourself. It's easy enough when you get the hang of it. We've just lost the hang. And now it's time to get it back. The hang, that is. Excuse me for half an hour or so.

I CAN BRING MEDITATION TO LIFE NOW

That's better.

As I was sitting here, I thought of my grandad. When we were on holiday together, he'd rise at 5 a.m. and go up to the beach hut and make himself a cup of tea; he'd sit there, just drinking his tea and looking out to sea. During the day, he'd sit in his deckchair, smiling, and not saying much. When he said anything, it was generally appreciative: of the sound of the seagulls or the warmth of the day, or the tastiness of a cheese and pickle sandwich.

He wasn't meditating. He wasn't doing gratitude practice. He wasn't being mindful. He wasn't practising kindness. He was just sitting still for hours and appreciating life, as it is. Here's how to get the hang of that (again?)

THE THREE MODES OF THE MIND

Last year, while sitting still and looking out to sea one day (it's genetic, you see), I realized that, when we're not in conversation with someone, or we're not being distracted by something or other, our minds are in one of three modes.

Now, I could multiply the number of modes to incorporate sometimes subtle differences in mode, but keeping it simple, and to three, works for me – and it's worked for all those I've shared this with over the past year.

Mode 1

The first mode is when we're thinking about something, and we're so involved in that thought process that you could say we're 'lost' in those thoughts. This is likely to be the default mode of your own particular head.

The thoughts could be about anything: going over things from the past, planning or worrying about things in the future, or pondering what to have for lunch (a ham and cheese focaccia, thanks for asking). Or how, if you skip lunch (I won't, thanks), you might lose a bit of your belly (no I won't, I'm afraid).

Mode 2

The second mode is when you're aware of your thoughts in some way. So that might be when you suddenly come out of a particular thought process and then look at that thought process in some way.

So you might think, *Oohh, look at me being so negative – why do I get like this?* It's as if another person enters the conversation. Given our earlier practice of noticing things more but trying to judge less, mode 2 might also include just emerging from your thoughts and simply noticing them.

There's also the possibility of being in a thought process and being aware of the thoughts – as if from the outside – simultaneously. So in mode 2, you might be thinking exactly the same thoughts as in mode 1, but you're aware of those thoughts too, as if from the outside, rather than being 'lost' in them.

Mode 3

This is the absence of thoughts. Some people find it difficult to imagine what the absence of thoughts could be like, as they don't think they've experienced it. And trying to imagine it, or wondering whether they've experienced it, doesn't really help.

But the more you're in mode 2, and are seeing how the thoughts work, the more you'll see there are small *gaps* between the thoughts (usually). And once you start to notice them, these gaps slowly start to grow, without any effort or intention on your part.

That's it: that's what happens in your head when you're not your phone.

So? Well, once you're aware of this, you just need to put the kettle on, make a cup of tea, and sit around, noticing which mode you're in, and how your head is working. And there's no aim to this: you're not aiming to increase the amount of mode 2, and then mode 3, that you experience. Let me repeat that: *there's no aim to this*. You're not aiming to increase the amount of mode 2, and then mode 3, that you experience. And no matter how many times I say that, many of you will want to do it, and think you've failed if you stay in mode 1.

But please, especially at the beginning, don't judge which mode you're in. Otherwise, you'll introduce tension to the exercise. Because whenever we want something, there's a tension around whether or not we'll get it.

Just creating the space to be still, and then being aware that there are these three modes, is enough to create some very interesting results. And it's likely too that, after a while, you'll simply start to enjoy the process (even more than looking at your phone).

Again, I know this from the retreat I ran on Stromboli this summer. Each time the group sat together, I'd give us a specific time to do so, which slowly increased over the course of the week. I'd time it precisely, too. So after, say, 15 minutes, I'd bring everyone back (not that they'd gone anywhere; they were actually more 'here' than ever before) and ask: 'Who would have been happy to sit for longer?' At the beginning of the retreat, only a couple of people put up their hand.

By the end of the week, most hands were up (so we were able to sit for ages). Why did some people not want to continue sitting, even at the end of the week? Three reasons: they were frustrated that they couldn't find more peace and get to mode 3 (that's why it's important not to be bothered which mode you're in); the thoughts they were having (generally in mode 1) weren't pleasant; or they just got bored. (The trick with boredom is simply to sit through it, like a runner going through their 'wall'.)

In fact, the trick with this whole thing is to try to sit it out, full stop. If you just carry on sitting – even if it's uncomfortable, or the thoughts are difficult, or you're bored – it usually all settles and resolves in time. It's distracting ourselves – and thus not facing those discomforts – that creates the problems.

LEVEL 2 FACT

Meditation is as good at reducing the symptoms of depression and anxiety as antidepressants.[2]

---

2 A 2014 review study by researchers at the USA's Johns Hopkins University School of Medicine looked at meditation and its efficacy in reducing stress-related symptoms like depression, anxiety, and pain. It found that the 'effect size' of meditation was 'moderate', at 0.3; however, the effect size of antidepressants is also 0.3, so the benefits of meditation rival those of pharmaceuticals.

MIND THE GAP

Now, only read this next bit if you've started to try this sitting-around-with-a-cup-of-tea-in-one-of-three-modes-thing. Once you can do it without judging which mode you're in, you can then move on to noticing how pleasant it is in mode 3 (or mode 2 for that matter).

And as you notice how pleasant it is, you'll naturally start to learn how to increase the gaps when there's nothing, or very little, going on in your head. After a while you might find that you can slip into these gaps at will, especially if you're relatively relaxed, and that they last for increasing amounts of time.

You may be wondering how you'll know when you're in a gap, if it really is a complete cessation of thinking. I've asked lots of people about their experience of the gaps, and it seems that, for some, there's no thinking and no separate awareness during them; they only know that there's been a gap as they come out of it. This makes mode 3, for them, more like mode 1: in that they are 'lost' in the gap.

For me, and for others, there's an awareness in the gaps. It feels as if there's a watching, but no commenting. For me, it's like watching myself gently holding my breath, and the breath then gently returns occasionally (as the thoughts return). This makes mode 3 more like mode 2.

And – really don't read this next bit until you've been sitting around like this for a while – I'll share too what I was doing for myself when

I first developed this idea (or observation) a year ago. I'd sit with my stopwatch (or rather, my watch in 'stopwatch' mode), with my finger poised over the 'start' button, and I'd start the timer when I hit a gap. I'd then see how long the gap would be. And I could, very soon, easily increase the gaps' duration.

It's a great way of training your brain to drop into such gaps (and thus... peace). But I am, as you've seen, very reluctant to share this, because having that as the aim of the exercise – to get to the mode 3 gaps and to increase them – is likely to reduce the all-round pleasure of sitting. And it's likely to increase tension.

It could easily become like a meditation boot camp. And, like any boot camp, it might do you some good for a while, but soon you can't wait to get back to sitting on your sofa with a beer in one hand and your phone in the other.

In fact, if you've got this far, and only did so by practising sitting around, then this is the higher-level trick for the whole sitting-around thing: how can you hold the idea that all modes are just the same – that it's no better being in mode 3 than in mode 1 – while, at exactly the same time, gently guiding yourself into mode 2 and then mode 3. Preferably without a stopwatch.

The ability to do apparently opposing things at the same time – and thus create, and hold, a paradox – will, as you'll see later, become possibly the most interesting and enlightening aspect of the whole thing.

Right, it's time for another cup of tea for me. It's early and no one's about; I'm out on the balcony of our broken villa and the sea is lapping the shingly shore. So I'm just going to sit around now until the family world wakes up and gets going…

… And I realized as I was sitting here just now (and as various members of our two families arrived at this, now breakfast, table) that I hadn't said anything more about the title of this section, 'I can bring meditation to life now'.

Because, if you want to, you can see the modes 1–3 process as 'meditation'. If so, it's a form of meditation that everyone can do. But calling it 'meditation' limits it, and separates it from life, for me. As I said, my grandad wasn't meditating, he was just sitting around, drinking tea.

So I'd prefer to see it as just a part of life, or – if *you* prefer – a way to bring meditation to life. And, as you can probably see, that has two potential meanings: a way to take your meditation practice out into life, and a way to enliven a form of meditation.

Rather than meditation, I'm just going to call the next section 'I can sit and drink tea now, and be at peace'. Ready? Watch…

I CAN SIT AND DRINK TEA NOW, AND BE AT PEACE

Sitting around and drinking tea is, for me, the most effective way to access peace in life. We're now going to look at how you can further play with this experience and how you can create more opportunities to sit around and drink tea.

I WANT TO DRINK MORE TEA NOW

If you're able to sit around in modes 1, 2 or 3 (without caring so much which one you're in), you'll soon really start to enjoy it. And when you enjoy something, you naturally want to do more of it. So really feel that enjoyment, when it happens (and it won't happen all the time, as I've mentioned). Then, without much effort, you'll start to find lots of ways to sit around more, drinking tea (if that does indeed become your thing).

Imagine if you enjoyed just sitting looking out of the window as much as you enjoy talking to a friend on the phone. Imagine if, on your drive to work, you enjoyed sitting in the car in silence as much as having the radio on, or listening to your favourite driving playlist. Imagine sitting on the loo and not reading a magazine or looking at your phone, and instead, getting into mode 2 as you do your number two.

You'll know it when it starts to happen. And it *will* start to happen. And when it does, rejoice, as you're now naturally finding more peace in your life.

LEVEL 2 HACK

No matter how blissful your experience
of peace, don't hang onto it and
never try to recreate it: flush it down
the loo with your next (blissful) poo.

I'LL DO LESS, SO I CAN DRINK MORE TEA

As you begin to enjoy sitting around and drinking tea, and the opportunities to do so multiply naturally, as if out of nowhere, you'll also probably want to make some deliberate moves to do less and sit around more. And this is when one word in particular comes in very handy: *no*.

You'll probably start saying no to invitations, to evening classes, to long conversations, to overtime at work, to box-set-binging, to non-essential chores, as you take the other option: just sitting around and drinking tea.

If that starts to concern you – and you think you'll lose all your friends and become Billy no-mates – consider the new quality you'll bring to everything you do outside those sitting-around moments. As you make contact with and get to know this more peaceful side of yourself, imagine how different you'll be when you do get on the phone to a friend, or you go to a party, or you're in an important meeting at work, or you're doing the washing-up.

Indeed, the more you get into sitting around and drinking tea, the more everything else in your life will begin to feel like sitting around and drinking tea. In doing so, might you naturally arrive at Level 3 on your own? We'll see.

I'LL AUTOMATE MY LIFE AND DRINK MORE TEA

You're more likely to get this sensation of sitting around and drinking tea, even when you're not sitting around and drinking tea, when you're involved in tasks that don't require a vast amount of intellectual exertion.

I'm not necessarily suggesting that you resign from your job as a professor of political science and go and work in the local factory packing tins into boxes. Though my happy, grateful and naturally meditative grandad did just that (not the resigning the professorship bit, but some form of tins-into-boxes factory task).

No, but whatever you do, it's likely that you can simplify it and organize it more. I use the word 'automate' in the title of this section, because I know a good deal about how to literally automate parts of your life: I automate a good deal of marketing and customer service tasks in our business, for example.

No, and I've started another paragraph with 'no', even though I've moved on from the point about using 'no': I'm talking about a variety of things you can do to reduce your effort and willpower exertion. For example, if I carefully plan what I have to do on a working day, at the beginning of that day, it frees me up during the rest of the day to just go ticking through my list.

Having to follow my list, which tells me 'one hour of emails', *tick*, then 'one hour of accounts', *tick*, then 'one hour, write blog', *tick*, frees me up and relaxes me a lot more than doing one task then trying to figure out what it's best to do next.

The same goes for just about anything in your life: 'automate' the bits that would unnecessarily waste energy and effort. That way, more and more of your life will start to feel like sitting around, drinking tea.

LEVEL 2 HACK

Always end a 'meditation' session with some mediation, mastication or masturbation. It keeps things lively and reminds you that mixing up your life is as important (and easy) as mixing up words.

I CAN INCREASE THE NATURAL EFFECT OF DRINKING TEA

I'm happy that, by now, you've probably been sitting around and drinking tea a good deal yourself. You should therefore know what it feels like to be more peaceful. Well, for you, anyway. I'm aware that relaxing and being more peaceful feels different for different people. When teaching retreats I have to be careful not to assume that my experience of peace is the same as everyone else's.

The more you get to know what peace feels like for you, the more peace you'll be able to access. For example, when I relax and become more peaceful, I become more sensitive to sound. I notice sounds more, and the sounds reassure me and relax me more.

I'm writing this on another idyllic sand-duney beach on the southwest coast of Sicily, so as I relax now (which is easy, of course), the sound of the waves and of chattering friends and children, and of the wind blowing our sun umbrella and the pages of this notebook, all rise to the surface of my consciousness.

I feel even more relaxed, and listening to the sounds does something to me that often happens when I become more peaceful: it brings back happy memories (usually from childhood). So, for me, a familiar and happy chain reaction occurs in my brain when I start to relax. But that's me. And knowing this – observing this – means that I can use sounds to help myself become more peaceful when I need to.

What happens to you? How do relaxation and peace feel for you? What happens in your body, and in your mind? As you begin to observe this, make a mental note (in a relaxed fashion) for later. Because what you experience when you're peaceful can subsequently be used to make you more peaceful when you're not. This is the fundamental trick of relaxation exercises: to use the 'effects' of relaxation to engender relaxation whenever you want, and need, to relax.

This is how I've generally taught relaxation over the years. But, as I mentioned earlier, there's an even better shortcut: just relax... just feel more peaceful at the drop of a hat. So drop that hat and let the tea go to your (hat-less) head.

LEVEL 2 FACT

At the University of California, Los Angeles, USA, researchers have found that the Buddhist-inspired Mindfulness-Based Stress Reduction programme, which includes meditation, improves immune function.[3]

TEA GOES TO YOUR HEAD

When you sit around and drink tea – in fact, when you find more peace in any way – your brain, and a whole lot more, changes. The predominant behaviour of Level 1 living – planning, striving, hurrying and achieving – is, to be rather simplistic about how the brain works, predominantly left hemisphere.

And when we relax, we switch more to the right hemisphere. Of course, the real picture is somewhat more complicated, with the brain changing in frequency too, and different areas of the left and right hemispheres lighting up, both individually and simultaneously.

Broadly speaking, though, we associate the left brain with logic, language, rationality, planning, and future- and past-based thinking; and the right brain with creativity, openness, presence, calm and peacefulness.

---

3   Source: Dr Daniel J. Siegel, 'The Science of Mindfulness'; www.mindful.org/the-science-of-mindfulness/

The movement then from the Level 1 behaviour of imagining that we can be at peace and happy one day in the future to the Level 2 realization that we can be peaceful now, is a movement from left to right brain. And that's generally a very good thing.

It's also a movement in the nervous system: from sympathetic to parasympathetic. Again, this is somewhat simplistic, but the sympathetic system is the 'alert and ready' system – always looking for the threat and poised to fight or flee – and the parasympathetic system is the resting and restorative system. And, again, that's generally a very good thing. And talking of good things...

TEA IS GOOD FOR YOU

For many reasons, sitting and drinking tea, being more at peace, and then creating changes in the brain and body, are very good for you.

Western science and medicine tends to focus on the detrimental effects of stress and tension on the body and brain. There's a vast amount of evidence for the numerous diseases and conditions that are either created or exacerbated by stress. The emphasis, then, is on how to avoid stress, rather than on how to encourage relaxation and peace.

Eastern medicine, in the form of a discipline like Traditional Chinese Medicine (TCM), also recognizes that stress and tension are a major cause of disease, but it also places great emphasis on relaxation (in the form of meditation and healing arts like Qigong) for its healing potential.

From the perspective of Level 2, when you realize that you can actually be at peace now, and that life can improve now – not in a month or a year, or a lifetime – there's the (not insignificant) benefit that you'll be significantly healthier, which will help prevent illness.

But we all know this, don't we?

I LOVE TEA, BUT...

I do love sitting around and drinking tea. I do love feeling at peace with myself and the world. It feels as if everything will turn out OK, no matter what's happening in the news, and life, headlines.

I'm able to sit around and just enjoy being me: watching the world, and my thoughts, go by. Nothing needs to be done to feel OK. Nothing needs to be said. I don't need to go anywhere, or be anything else, or improve, or heal, or resolve, to feel at peace.

In this sense of peace, my body is relaxed and soft, and my head feels clearer and lighter. I tend to be funnier too: more playful and less inhibited. Crucially, things don't matter so much. What I thought were problems seem further away from here.

From here, and I'm here now as I write this, the colours are more vivid and the sounds more evocative; the tastes are more precise and delicious, and the sense of just being alive is... tangibly and gently... THRILLING.

If only I could be here all the time...

BUT I CAN'T REMAIN AT PEACE FOR LONG (THERE'S ALWAYS SOMETHING)

Are you familiar with the following phenomenon? Something bad has happened – maybe you've lost someone close to you – but somehow you manage to get to sleep. When you wake up, everything is fine with the world, for a few moments, but then the realization hits you like a train. And you're back into your grief and pain.

Similarly, it seems that, no matter how good we are at feeling peace in the present – no matter how good our techniques, or how good we become at just sitting around and drinking tea – something always pops up and drags us out of that state of peace. And it doesn't have to be anything big, either.

It just seems that, no matter how old we are, or how good or bad our health, or how successful or wealthy we are, or whichever country and climate we live in, or how blessed, or not, we are in various ways...

There's always something...

THE FAMILY SOMETHING

If you've ever had a relative, you'll know that there's *always* something of a family nature going on. Perhaps you're worried about your kids, or jealous of your sibling, or feel 'unheard' by your parents, or are unhappy with your partner; whether there's a genuine family crisis or the 'something' that's going on has been bubbling away for most of your life, this particular something is so peace-disturbing because it's (literally) so close to home – and because it's more difficult to opt out of.

As we'll see, in many cases, if something is really disturbing you, you can choose to leave that situation. And there are clearly many people who leave relationships, and families with kids, and those who break off contact with parents and siblings.

But we're more attached in family relationships: it's not like losing contact with a friend. When something goes wrong, or there are disagreements, or familiar and disturbing dynamics, it's harder to find our peace, as it all feels like it means too much.

THE MONEY SOMETHING

Sometimes the 'family something' is a 'money something': we know a few families who are, at the moment, stressing and arguing over inheritance issues. There's nothing like someone dying and leaving something different to different people to stir things up.

Maybe you could do with a little inheritance yourself at the moment, to ease any money tensions that you have? It's hard to be at peace when you're unsure whether you can pay the rent or mortgage this month. Or when you're struggling to keep your business afloat; or when the stock market has just crashed and taken your net worth with it; or when house prices have gone up again, making the prospect of owning your own home increasingly unlikely.

We covered money in Level 1 – 'I'll be at peace when...' – but the peace-delaying activity of that level is different to the peace-interrupting effects of Level 2. These concerns are more immediate. It's less 'I'll be at peace when I've paid off the mortgage,' and more, 'I would feel at peace if it wasn't for this high mortgage payment I have to make this month.'

The money something is particularly peace-interrupting because money issues branch out into so many areas of our lives, and are often related to our basic needs and very survival. When we're struggling with money, we're struggling with our rent or mortgage (shelter), our bills (heat and light), our food costs (sustenance) and our leisure costs, such as going out or taking a holiday (rest). It's clearly hard to feel at peace when it seems our very survival is under threat.

THE GEO-POLITICAL SOMETHING

Speaking of survival, as you know I'm writing this in the summer of 2017, when Donald Trump is goading the leader of North Korea with threats of 'fire and fury'. Commentators are calling it 'this generation's Cuban missile crisis'. People are scared.

Although we are holidaying – sitting on dream beaches, swimming in the warm sea (which today is unusually rough and thus great for wave jumping and body surfing) – I wake each day somewhat dreading reading the news: what Trump has said or done overnight, scaring the shit out of us from a golf cart. Though I still feel strangely compelled to read every word on every angle of this crisis. It's hard to be at peace, even on holiday, when everyone is openly talking about nuclear war.

I'm aware too that, by the time you read this, you'll know how this particularly grim chapter turned out. Maybe it all blew over and you've forgotten about it. Or maybe it all blew up, in every sense, and it's changed everything.

As I read more commentary and opinion on the current crisis, the 'war of words', I can tell that I'm actually looking for something to reassure me. But it's hard to find. I feel like a gambler who, having lost a lot at the table (in my case, the peace-of-mind table), keeps betting in order to win it all back.

Like any gambler, I do occasionally win something back: yesterday I read the views of three experts on North Korea, who all said they thought the prospect of actual military conflict was highly unlikely. I breathed a small sign of relief, until my breath was promptly taken away again by another belligerent tweet from President Trump.

There is, of course, something absurd – and I would like to say comical – about this crisis, but it feels too heavy for that now, as we gallop towards the apocalypse with this buffoon. It's like being led off a cliff by Benny Hill, all of us running in single file, speeded up, with that music playing (if you know it, you're now singing it in your head).

So I sit on this beach and I breathe. I take in the astonishing view. I lie down and have a nap. I wake up feeling rested and at peace; and then I think of Donald.

At the geo-political level, there's always something – and it seems like a particular drawn-out, existential-threat-something now. I hope we can get through this orange-stained-Trump-something soon and without too much loss of life.

THE HEALTH SOMETHING

A common peace-disturber for me is my health. Or rather, the not-health bits. I seem to suffer from two opposing and equal mental afflictions: the first is the belief that I'm invincible and could survive anything, even a bullet in the guts (I've had that particular fantasy since I was a boy and watched too many Westerns); and the second is the delusion that once I'm ill, I'll never get better.

I was 12 when I first experienced the second delusion (well, *so far* it's been a delusion: I'm aware that one day it will turn out to be true). I'd been sent home from school with the flu, and I felt terrible – I really couldn't imagine feeling anything other than that terrible ever again in my life.

If I'm feeling peaceful – as I am at the moment, our boys having emerged from a thrilling surf session in the sea – and all seems well with the world (if I don't bring to mind the orange-topped warmonger), it only takes a twinge in my right knee, as I get up, to curtail that sense of peace. I start wondering whether that pain will be there *every* time I get up, for the rest of my life, or whether it will get worse. Then I imagine failed surgery that leaves me forever limping.

I'm exaggerating – I normally just say to myself, *I must get that checked out by the physio* – but the worry is there, lurking in every unknown cause of the slightest ache or pain. And it's a worry that always drifts me away from my peaceful state, like the gentle cross-shore current that's right in front of me now: the one that, every 10 minutes or so, forces me to walk against it to get back to my original position in front of the beach umbrella (thus straining my knee).

Knee ache, hip ache, headache, enflamed this, irritable that; a rash here, an itch there – with a limp, a fart, a faint and a flutter, there's always something, health-wise.

THE WEATHER SOMETHING

In theory, I should be struggling to write this one, as we live in Italy, where the weather is generally something to celebrate rather than complain about.

I'm British and the stereotype is that we spend a lot of time talking, and complaining, about the weather – and with good reason. But I've found that the Italians, too, talk a lot about the weather. Granted, not as much as they talk about food...

In Italy, most meals are spent talking about food, which sounds rather reasonable as I write it, but I'm simply not accustomed to it. At mealtimes, most Anglo-Saxons talk about something *over* their food, not about the food itself. But maybe that's simply because there's not as much to talk about as there is over an Italian meal.

It's *Ferragosto* today. This is Italy's big public holiday on 15 August, when the whole country goes to the beach, and then out for a big meal where they talk about how marvellous the food is. We've just enjoyed (and I *mean* enjoyed) three fresher days, with a breeze, a more turbulent sea and lower temperatures (average 34°C/93°F). So everyone was talking about that.

Today we're probably back into the high 30°Cs, maybe low 40°Cs, and everyone will be talking about how hot it is, and how impossible it is to do anything – apart from going into the sea or lying down. My peace was disturbed, even this morning, as I was trying to do Qigong on the beach at 8:30 a.m. (rather than a more sensible 7:30 a.m.) and it was just too hot. I would be literally more peaceful if it wasn't for this (gorgeous) weather.

No, we have nothing to complain about here. But my compatriots and friends in less hospitable climes do. If, after a long, dark winter, your summer is generally cloudy and wet, then it can feel harder to be at peace with the world. Particularly during the specific times that you try to catch up on peace – your holidays. No matter how good we've become at putting up with the rain, we'd (generally) prefer the sun.

THE ME SOMETHING

Even when the weather's perfect, and all the other life conditions are apparently ideal – if indeed that ever happens – there's usually something that rises up within us to disturb our peace: the dreaded 'me' something. The Buddhist saying 'wherever you go, there you are' sums this up rather depressingly.

It's often a blessed relief that there are enough other 'somethings' in life to mask the fact that, if you could clear everything of an external nature that disturbs your peace, you'd still have something arising within *you* to do the job.

You can call this something whatever you want: 'issues', 'problems', 'attachment issues', 'unresolved trauma', 'character flaws' – yikes – it doesn't change the fact that there's always something. So, having found yourself beautifully at peace with the world in a good session of sitting around and drinking tea, it usually doesn't take long for something to trigger you, or upset you, or make you feel inadequate, or oversensitive.

It doesn't take long for you to start comparing yourself to others (usually harshly), or feeling sorry for yourself, or wondering what you did wrong, and feeling guilty, even shameful.

I know I'm touching my 'me something' when I say something not so pleasant to myself, like: 'you prat'. It happened recently, during a trip to the UK. I was staying in a hotel near the airport I'd arrived at the day before ('London' Southend, I'm almost ashamed to say) and decided to send a text message to my friend Simon, arranging for us to meet up.

I wanted to get online with my laptop, but there was no Wi-Fi code written anywhere in my room. There was also no phone, but I found the number for the hotel using my own phone. So I noted down two numbers on a piece of paper: Simon's, so I could send him a text, and the hotel's number, so I could ask how to get on Wi-Fi.

I checked the numbers and then texted Simon. I then re-consulted the piece of paper and tapped in the number for the hotel's reception desk. A man answered immediately, saying, 'Good morning.' 'Good morning to you,' I replied. 'I was wondering if and how I can access Wi-Fi in my room – do I need a code or something?'

'A Wi-Fi code?' the man on the reception desk asked. 'Yes,' I said, 'a Wi-Fi code, so I can access the Wi-Fi.' It was as if he'd never been asked this before, which surprised me, what with this being a hotel and there being no Wi-Fi code displayed in the room, or printed on the small card pouch that came with my room card.

And then the receptionist burst into laughter. I was shocked, affronted. Is he drunk, I thought? Has he been up all night, and is just tired? How could he laugh at me for making such a reasonable request? I felt like I was at school.

Then, as he burst into another round of laughter, I realized I recognized the tones, the timbre, of the laugh. *Crikey, I must know this person*, I thought. I wondered whether I'd hit the wrong 'contact' on my phone, as you sometimes do. My brain scanned through my male friends: who could this be?

Then I realized (as you probably have already) – it was Simon. I'd dialled *his* number from my handwritten note, not the hotel's. We laughed about it – it was fun. And at some level I don't care about such things. But there's still that level which, after I'd put the phone down, made me say to myself, *you total prat*, and then punch my own head.

I now pause and realize that I've just exposed another embarrassing episode in my life; and I say to myself, *you prat*. I have, though, managed to namecheck Simon; I mentioned him in my book *F**k It, Do What You Love*, but he never read about himself there. And, even though I told him I'd probably mention him again in this book, he probably won't read this one either. Prat.

The truth is that we've all gone through stuff in our lives that has left its mark. However well-intentioned our parents, guardians, teachers and guides were (and clearly some of them weren't), few of us were ideally loved, cherished, protected and guided through our early years. Few of us were seen as the perfect, whole, angelic beings we were (and are), but instead were projected upon, and moulded in others' images.

We can, of course, slowly work through the issues that we have, the patterns that hold us back, and the marks that have been left. And that can be a beautiful (and painful) process. But it doesn't change the fact that, even when we find we're at peace, we usually find, soon enough, there's some 'me' something or other.

THE ENVIRONMENT
SOMETHING

In 1989, the world was changing (and I was changing too: leaving university to enter the big wide world). The Cold War was over, and we celebrated as the wall came down in Berlin. For years we'd lived in the shadow of a possible nuclear apocalypse, and then that threat fell away. I celebrated for a day, and the next day I realized we were heading for an environmental apocalypse. Looking back, I don't know whether I enjoyed that day of celebration and peace quite enough.

I educated myself about the growing threat of global warming; I joined Friends of the Earth and Greenpeace, and other charities whose names I can't now recall, my monthly donations to them having long since lapsed. But I mainly experienced a period of gloom and pessimism.

Today, close to 30 years later, I walk on a beach strewn with washed-up plastic detritus; I recall from a recent news story that the accumulation of plastic waste around the world could soon pose a threat as great as the planet's warming. And another story, just yesterday, revealed that scientists are detecting tiny bits of plastic in fish – and even in our tap water. Plastic has entered the food chain, and thus our bodies.

In a relatively short period of time – given how long we've been on this planet, and how long this planet existed before we arrived – we've really messed things up. We're at a critical point now: we all know that (even those who still try to deny the overwhelming scientific evidence).

It's easy to be gloomy about the state of the Earth and our environment – about its future, and our future. So, when we're feeling at peace with the world, it's easy to be pulled out of that sense of peace when we remember what we're doing to that world.

THE WORK SOMETHING

I was sitting on the balcony of our holiday villa last night, listening to the sound of the waves crashing onto the shore: just sitting, enjoying sitting. And then my phone beeped with some notification or other (I haven't yet learned which sounds relate to which subject I'm being notified of). Ha, my phone just 'notified' me of something else as I was typing that...

Last night the notification was a message from a member of our F**k It team, who was telling me about an issue with a retreat booking. I thought about the issue for a few minutes, worried a bit, then came up with an answer, and messaged her back. Gaia and I have had our own business – running retreats and various courses – for 14 years now. And there's always something...

Now, I'm generally accustomed to dealing with the numerous somethings, and I know what I'm happy to be 'disturbed' by on holiday;

our team is great at covering most of the numerous somethings, but they'll contact me when a particular kind of something comes up. This was one of those, so the team member was right to send the message; however, it doesn't alter the fact that this particular moment of peace was disturbed by that particular work something.

So, whether you have your own business too, or you're freelance, or you're employed, or you're just checking out the value of your stock portfolio on your phone every morning, there's always something with work and business. Always.

THE UNCLEAR SOMETHING

On this holiday we're on at the moment, with two other families, we're experiencing the effects of a lack of clarity. And this is very familiar to me.

In my birth family, we believed that everything was happy and smiley (and 'clappy' too, if you take into account the evangelical Christian backdrop to it all), but beneath the surface there was a world of feeling and thinking that wasn't expressed verbally.

The thing is, even when things aren't said, they are *felt*. So the dynamics that ensue with a lack of clarity and expression include: judgement, suspicion, resentment, feeling 'wrong', power games, silent bullying, and tensions and blocks in many ways. Such blocked dynamics tend to create illness and unhappiness, even if you're still smiling (and clapping) on the surface.

The lack of clarity we're experiencing and observing at the moment has created huge tensions. Taking the step to express the unexpressed and say the unsaid takes courage. It's rarely easy or painless to confront difficulties and bring them out into the open.

There are two competing expressions that allude to this: 'clearing the air' and 'airing your dirty laundry'. Though I suspect what connects them, and takes us to the same place, is that airing our dirty laundry will ultimately lead to a clearing of the air too (and the dirty laundry will be 'aired' and thus cease to pollute the space).

It is, apparently, easier to not say anything and just carry on. An alternative to the famous and now overused wartime slogan 'Keep calm and carry on' would be 'Keep schtum and carry on'. That's what most of us do; we keep schtum (silent). But a lack of clarity in any relationship sends out ripples that will inevitably disturb your pond of peace.

THE DYING SOMETHING

When we find peace, and find ourselves at peace, the world is a beautiful place. The smallest and most ordinary things can give us joy: we appreciate life more than ever and feel the vibrancy of life, both in ourselves and out in the world.

So the realization that life is followed by death is a hard and often peace-dissolving one. Death and dying provide a rude interruption to our life-affirming sense of peace. And they do so in many ways: from the death of those we love and the demise of celebrities we adore (have you noticed that more of our beloved stars are dying at the moment?) and from the various forms of illness in ourselves and others that remind us of our mortality, to accidents, and the decay we see in nature. Even the down cycle of a business or the economy can remind us that everything tends towards decay and entropy.

It seems too that, by finding more peace in our lives – and by creating more space and relaxing more – we do get more in touch with the flipside of life. What a neat little euphemism that is; in fact, I think it's one of the reasons that many people don't, underneath it all, *want* to find space: they're scared of touching and feeling the flipside of their lives.

The truth is, there's always some 'dying' something. We can't avoid it. We can only try to ignore it, if that's our way (I hope it's not mine). This book is called (as you know) *F**k It. Be at Peace with Life, Just As It Is*, and it should really be called *F**k It. Be at Peace with Life and Death, Just As They Are*.

But hey, that's for Level 3. Here, in the dying embers of Level 2, death-related somethings serve only to jolt us from our happy-and-at-peace moments.

LEVEL 3

F**K IT.
BE AT PEACE
WITH LIFE,
JUST AS IT IS

F**k It is the gateway to Level 3. When you say F**k It, when you feel F**k It, when you live more F**k It, you naturally start to enter Level 3. And a big part of that is the effect F**k It has on how much we care.

F**K IT TO CARING

In both Levels 1 and 2, caring is a problem. In Level 1, because we care about having our own home, we believe that we'll only be at peace when we have one. In Level 2, if we have a house, a drop in property prices disturbs our peace because we care about its value.

In fact, caring is so often the root of our state of stress: it's such a rapid dissolver of peace that it might seem as if being at peace, and caring about stuff, are incompatible. Fortunately, though, it's how *much* we care, not caring *per se* that matters (so we *should* care about stuff, but not too much).

Caring too much and about too many things, is the path to pain. There's simply too much to go wrong, and too much at stake.

Imagine that you care deeply about your children (not much imagination is needed there if you have children, I suppose), and your position at work, and staying fit and well, and the state of the environment, and the price of gold; and that you also care about retaining liberal values in society, and upholding human rights, and that there are no further hikes in energy prices, and that combustion engines are phased out as soon as possible, and that your pension will keep you in the manner to which you've become accustomed, and so on.

Being at peace with all those cared-for-but-fragile spinning plates is going to be difficult (and you only need look behind that plate-spinning Greek restaurant down the road to the perpetually perilous state of its proprietors' home country to see how fragile things can be).

Equally, imagine not caring at all about anything. That's not an expression of the life force that arises when we find peace, is it? It's usually the opposite: an expression of depression. That's not the answer. Part of the answer is to care less about lots of things – hopefully the things that you realize don't actually matter so much to you.

That's an essential element of the power of F★★k It. When we say F★★k It we recognize that what we're caring so much about, but which is causing us pain, doesn't actually matter so much. In saying F★★k It to anything, we consciously and literally reduce our level of care for that thing.

Try it now: say F**k It to anything that's bothering you, and feel your care level reduce.

My favourite analogy for illustrating this point about care levels is the tachometer, or revometer: the gauge in your car that measures the engine's revolutions per minute. Or, in technical terms, 'revs per min'; or, to get even more technical, 'RPM'.

Are you still with me? I don't know if you ever look at, or use, that gauge, but there will be a point at which your car's engine is most comfortable, and then a point at which it will strain and lose power. That's the 'red line' and it's usually marked with, wait for it, a red line, or a red shaded area.

Your care levels are like this tachometer. If you care too much about too many things, you'll be straining and stressing about life too much. Whereas if you can reduce your care levels, you can get to a point where things are more comfortable. My car is most comfortable at 1,500 revs per minute, and my life is most comfortable at an equivalently low rate of cares per day.

Note too that if the revs in your car drop too low then you can lose power completely, and stall: and it's the same in life, as we stall into depression when we care for nothing at all. Getting your 'cares per day' rate lower, then, is critical to increasing your chances of peace. And F**k It will aid that, big time.

But I said this was *part* of the answer, and this is Level 3 after all. Level 3 takes F**k It up a level: so that we say F**k It to caring about caring. In doing so we recognize that there are times when we'll care too much – and things we'll care too much about – even though it's generally best to reduce those overall care levels.

Again, this is 'F**k It to caring' and also, at the same time, 'F**k It, I care: that's life.'

F**K IT TO POSITIVITY

We all know it's better to be positive, optimistic and life-affirming than it is to be negative, pessimistic and down. We want to be around people like that, and we want to be people like that. There's plenty of evidence that positive and optimistic people do better in life too, and attract more opportunities. But you don't need any 'evidence' for that, do you? It's obvious.

If you train yourself to be generally positive, you're at Level 2: when we realize that we can be positive and optimistic now, and that this can make a real and transforming difference to our lives (it really can, I'm positive). But, just as with our 'at peace state', life can drag us out of our positivity; and our natural selves can also sabotage our carefully practised positivity.

So Level 3 is F**k It to positivity. You don't have to be positive and optimistic all the time. Even if you were a positivity saint, there would be days when your halo would slip and you'd say: 'Oh, bloody hell, I knew that halo wouldn't last – it was probably made in China. What am I going to do now? I'll never find another halo at this time of year – the halo shops will be right out of haloes. Bloody typical.'

Yes, F**k It to positivity and optimism. You can give in to your inner grump, your Eeyore within. Don't resist, and see how much better you feel. Because it's more real and truthful that way. Give in to your inner grump today, and you'll naturally return to a more positive state tomorrow. But the movement is then natural and not forced.

Sure, it's better to be positive than negative. What, John? Can you stop contradicting yourself? One minute you're saying it's better to give in to your inner grump, the next, that it's better not to?' Well, yes and no, because:

Level 1: I'll be positive when...

Level 2: I can be positive now.

Level 3: It's fine to be as we are, whatever we are – positive or negative.

And I'm going to introduce a concept now that will serve us well until the end of this book, and possibly to the end of this life.

It's called 'We Have Two Hands'. To elaborate, we have two arms, and at the end of them, two hands. And as well as enabling us to carry out many tasks (such as holding our phone with one hand and typing into it with the other), the two-hands thing is rather useful in that it allows us to say, 'On the one hand (insert argument)', but on the other hand (insert counter-argument)'.

So, with our new handy little concept fully, errrmmm, grasped, this is how to apply it:

* On the one hand, of course it's better to be positive and optimistic than negative and pessimistic; and it's better to be Level 2 than 1.

* But on the other hand, it's perfectly natural to be negative and pessimistic at times, and the last thing you want to do is suppress something that's perfectly natural. When we allow what's natural within us, things keep moving. It's only when we make something 'wrong' – as we might make 'negativity' wrong at Level 2 – that things start to get stuck.

If we open the door to our own natural occasional grumpiness, we open the door to our own natural positivity at the same time. So nothing is forced: we're not forcing the grumpiness out, and we're not having to force the positivity in. And we all know what forced positivity looks and feels like – we speak optimistically through gritted teeth, and our smile is fixed and false.

So this is Level 3 – 'F**k It to positivity' and let's be real.

F**K IT TO BEING GOOD

Are you a good girl or boy? I am (the boy bit). I always have been. I did as I was told; I did my homework on time and stood up for the bullied kids at school; I raised money for charity and helped people across the road; if I knocked another car with my car door, I left a note for the driver; I handed lost items in to the police; I sent birthday and Christmas cards: I was a hard-working employee and then an understanding boss. And, of course, I'll have this book written on time with most of the 'i's dotted and the 't's crossed.

As far as 'being good' is concerned then, I find it easy. Though I've been 'bad' too of course, as we all have (I'm not talking criminal activity here). And don't go thinking you'll get another list here. What goes on in Parkin's memory, stays in Parkin's memory.

Well, Level 3ers, F**k It to being good. And by that, I don't mean go out and raise hell, piss people off or hurt them, of course. As you know, it's better to be good than bad. But it's even better to welcome ourselves, as we are, without judging too much. This is about being kinder to ourselves, just as we are.

And then it's the same when it comes to others: live and let live. Don't judge so much. Unless what someone is doing is having a detrimental effect on you, or hurting others, stay out of their business.

As I was writing that, a young Italian man came wandering past us on this pretty-much deserted beach; he was wearing headphones and singing along loudly and out-of-tunely with the music (as you do). Everyone tutted, and I muttered 'prat' (as I do), even though he was gone in a moment, and harming no one.

In this context, I like US author and speaker Byron Katie's concept (outlined in her book *Loving What Is*) of what is 'our business'. She divides life into 'my business', 'your business' and 'God's business'. An efficient, and more peaceful, way to live is to realize where everything lies, and to stay in your own business (and thus not get into others' or God's business).

Let's say you and I are having a meal together on the outdoor terrace of a restaurant on the coast. What I eat is 'my business'; what you eat is 'your business'; and what the weather does while we're sitting on the terrace is 'God's business'.

So it's tedious for you if I have anything to say about what you eat ('Ooh good,' you say, 'then I'll have the burger and chips, followed by the "Death by Chocolate" dessert'). It's tedious for me if you have anything to say about what I choose to eat (I'll have the burger and chips anyway). And it's tedious for God, and a waste of our energy of course, if we have anything to say about his weather tricks.

It's the same, generally speaking, with whether people are being good or bad: it's their business. Right up until the moment it becomes my business. And it's the same, generally speaking, with whether I'm being good or bad. It's my business, sure, but it's also Level 3 business – where we're saying 'F**k It to being good'. Amen (for doing His business).

F**K IT TO BEING AUTHENTIC

'Authentic' is the new 'good'. While I was growing up, being 'good' and, at home in particular, not 'sinning' was all the rage. Back then, grown-ups wore beards and sandals and bleated on about love, peace and goodness.

Now the beards are back and everyone's bleating on about being 'authentic'. And with good reason, too. As I explained earlier, in muscle tests we're always stronger when we're being authentic in any area of our lives, than when we're not. Being authentic is about being in our 'truth' and the truth literally makes us stronger (muscle testing is essentially a truth-and-lies detector). So, for some high Level 2 performance, be authentic.

The thing is, I'd be *in*authentic if I didn't admit that I'm not always authentic. For 100 reasons, some noble, some not, there will be times when we're not authentic in any way. In fact, inauthenticity is the oil that keeps our social engines running. We'll all say that we're fine to hear the truth, when we're not; that we're happy to listen, when we're not; that things are 'alright', when they're not; that we think bums don't look big in certain items of clothing when they patently do (but that's fine and still rather attractive).

I'll do things in life that don't express the 'authentic me' (like the accounts), be things that aren't particularly authentic (like being patient when I'm boiling with frustration), and say things that I don't believe.

So, F**k It to being authentic all the time. If it's not the moment to be authentic, don't get hung up about it – and revel in your inauthenticity. I really mean that. LOL. Smiley.

F**K IT TO BEING PATIENT

It's noon on one of the days of our holiday. But we're still hanging around in our rental villa while the world outside swims and sunbathes and plays on the beach. I've given up trying to rouse the masses – to organize the rest of the day – and instead sit relaxing on our bed (and writing this, clearly). I switch between feeling I'd like to shout and throw things around and just sitting back and resigning myself to my (ever-delayed) fate.

Being patient – and I'm generally pretty patient – has served me well in life. Good things come to those who wait, after all. I've been good at waiting, and I've enjoyed many good things as a result.

But I've also been very impatient and frustrated at times, and it's driven me to force things through and shake people up. And as unpleasant as shouting and throwing things around is, it does create an effect – and, often, the results you want. I'm exaggerating, of course: I don't often shout and throw things around, but I do express my impatience and frustration clearly to people.

In the recipe of life, I'd propose 20% shouting and throwing things around, and 80% calmly talking things through and being patient. The main thing, though, is to have little judgement about which way you go. That's Level 3. See what feels right at the time, and then follow that, without any self-judgement. That's being at peace: allowing what feels right in the moment and just following that.

So F**k It to being patient (Level 2) or to being shouty and impatient, and simply embrace what feels right at the time.

F**K IT TO HOW IT'S SUPPOSED TO GO

Our plane is just about to take off: Ancona to London, two hours and six minutes. If it seems as if we spend most of our time on a beach or in a plane, it's not true: it's simply the opportunities I'm getting to write this summer.

We're tired: we've spent two days at home, washing (clothes) and writing (emails) and running (about). So now we intend to sit back and sleep for two hours. We have eye masks and neck cushions. But there are two toddlers behind us who are very excited, and are expressing their excitement with lots of high-pitched yelping – and by kicking out their little legs (against our little seats). Maybe this flight won't go as we supposed it would.

The holiday we've just returned from didn't, either. It was supposed to go like this, but it went like that. And the fact that it went like that contributed to our current tiredness. We were surrounded by, and involved in, a whole host of dynamics. It was hard work, emotionally at least. All that sitting around on the beach was lovely, but the confusing world of the unspoken was difficult.

Lots of things in my life have not gone as they were supposed to. I'm alive (good news), when it was a close shave a few times. I have two beautiful sons (good news), and I never imagined that I'd have kids. I've had unexpected crises (bad news), unjust shocks (bad news), and anaphylactic shocks (big bad news).

As I fly to the UK to commence another big project, I have ideas about how I'd like it all to go, of how it's supposed to go – with a good wind, a stable geo-political climate, some hard work and planning, and a good dose of luck. And I can, now, feel the attachment to how I would like it all to go, and how it's supposed to go.

Well, F**k It to how it's supposed to go. I hereby (attempt to) embrace how it goes – in real-time-unfolding-reality – rather than how it's *supposed* to go. It is, after all, the gap between how I want it to go, and how it actually goes, that will cause me pain. And to close that gap, I must simply accept more what happens, as it happens.

I say 'simply' in the way that a yoga teacher will ask you to, 1. Jump your legs out wide... *tick*. 2. Lean forwards from the hip, with arms limp... *tick*. 3. Allow your head to drop to the floor, and let it rest there... *What?* Saying that is simple enough; and it almost sounds simple when you hear it said so simply. But doing it, in reality, is a different thing entirely.

Acceptance, though, is a major part of 'being at peace' with things, isn't it? I haven't used that word so far because it instantly brings up the idea of being passive; as if accepting is a form of giving in. Well, it doesn't have to be (and in its pure, radical way, it's not).

Acceptance as most of us imagine it is Level 2 acceptance: working with calm acceptance of the things that trouble us, disturb us, that we're resisting, or which go against our plan for life. Then there's Level 3 acceptance, which is a higher level of acceptance (not just in my level-numbering system, but in every way) of all that unfolds, of all that is (even our localized resistance).

On the one hand (yes, back to our key two-hands concept), we can work with what we're resisting; on the other hand we can be fine with our multiple-resistance crimes. In this way, Level 3 is like a loving parent to the loved small child: accepting of all (or most) behaviours, traits and ticks. Whatever the loving parent sees (that would disturb just about anyone else), they say 'F**k It, I love you.'

So 'love' becomes like a hot knife that slides through the butter of resistance and judgement. If you could love yourself in the way you love your children (if you have them), you'd instantly be more at peace with yourself. If you could love life and all that arises in your window onto reality, you'd instantly be more at peace with life.

Oh dear, I've just looked at my notes for the title of the next section...

F**K IT TO LOVING

This F**k It thing can be like a strict Zen master: you know, the one who'll come and hit you with a stick if your attention wanders from your present awareness meditation. Just when I'd uncovered the utter power of 'love' and 'loving' to cut through all that resistance just now, I felt the sting of the stick on my back from Zen Master F**k It.

(And I won't go back and change that now, and we won't edit it later please, editor – because that shows how easy it is to slip back into Level 2.)

Because loving, of course, is in Level 2. Yes, it would be marvellous to be able to love ourselves and life just as we love our children. Just as it would be marvellous to be as peaceful in a traffic jam as we are when we're lying on a beach (and there are no family–friend dynamics going on in the background).

But extending that unconditional love beyond your own children is tough indeed. I have my mini-demonstrators of that sitting right behind me. No matter how hard I try, I cannot extend the unconditional love I feel for the two boys sitting next to me to the two little brats behind me who are screaming and kicking my seat. Of course I don't hold them in the contempt I reserve for their half-pissed parents – they're innocent children after all – but I do not love them in any way, I'm afraid.

So, F**k It to loving. And by that, I'm not proposing that we all start hating. Love when you can, how you can; spread the love; love yourself more – even the shouty kids behind you more, if you can – love life more. But don't get down on your non-loving self and behaviour either. That's Level 3. That's being at peace with how you are, as you are, and life, as it is.

F**K IT TO LOVING YOURSELF

At a therapeutic level, there's little you can do that's more powerful for self-healing than loving yourself more (and, ultimately, unconditionally).

We talk to ourselves, and treat ourselves, in a way that we'd rarely use to talk to, or treat, other members of the human race, even people we don't like. So on the one hand, if you want to improve things in your life, big time, at Level 2, then work on loving yourself more.

Louise Hay has (and I'm afraid that's now 'had', as she passed away between the time I wrote these words in a notebook and typed them into my laptop) the most beautiful affirmation at the heart of her 'Heal Your Life' teaching: 'I love and approve of myself.'

She suggested you say it to yourself 100 times a day. You'll encounter a good deal of resistance as you do this (because it's usually not true that you love and approve of yourself – yet, at least). But the light will slowly start to spread: shining into the dark, self-loathing corners of your own head, and then out into the world.

And, just as with a practice of peace, or acceptance, this self-loving regime will work and, eventually (probably) lead you naturally into Level 3: i.e. the realization that true self-love *includes* and even embraces the self-loathing.

So, F**k It to loving yourself – or, rather, believing that you should only love yourself – and seeing not loving yourself as somehow wrong. We don't really like 'somehow wrong' in Level 3, and 'not really liking' is just fine too.

F**K IT TO THE LINEAR PROCESS

In endeavouring to show you how being 'at peace' with life, just as it is, is very different from feeling peaceful, I've introduced the three levels of this book. The implicit suggestion in such a three-level model is that we can move through the levels in a linear way, so that attaining 'wisdom' would constitute the following process:

* Realizing that feeling at peace should be our highest aim.

* Believing that we'll feel at peace once the next thing has been attained.

* Realizing that we don't have to *wait* to feel at peace – we can feel it *now*.

* Seeing that there's always something to bring us out of peace.

* Recognizing that there's a higher level of being at peace that includes everything, including not being peaceful.

There's also an implicit suggestion that we can move through these levels by simply understanding intellectually how they work. But the reality of such wisdom attainment is likely to be very different. It's unlikely to happen in such a linear way (though it might) and it's unlikely to be attained through intellectual understanding alone (though that is conceivable).

So, as we draw nearer to the end of our Level 3 process, we're going to blast open both the linear aspect of the wisdom progression, and the emphasis on the intellectual understanding of it.

And an out-of-chronology diary entry will now assist us in this blasting: as I recount a random, seemingly unprompted moment of peace and clarity and then ponder the phenomenon of illumination.

Diary entry: 6 May 2017 – From *Mad Men* to Peaceful Man

It's late afternoon. Earlier, after a rather pleasant nap, I watched an episode of the US TV show Mad Men *on Netflix. And, just before that ended, 10 minutes ago, something rather peculiar happened. Not in the show's plot, but to me.*

I'd been sitting there watching the episode – enjoying watching the episode, if you know what I mean. My brain was taking several lines of thought during this pleasant watching experience, and one of them was how pleasant it was to be sitting there watching.

*Another was that I should really get on soon with continuing the job I'm currently doing (recording the audio sessions for the 'F**k It Sorts Stress eCourse' that starts on Tuesday). But I thought maybe I should start that after having a walk; because I haven't had a walk today, and it would be nice to have a walk before it gets dark.*

Then some slight guilt about sitting watching the television arose, and I told myself that it was a perfectly fine way to spend my time – it's Saturday afternoon after all – and that the work will get done one way or another. And I settled again.

These were the lines of thought that I suppose were arising in the less dramatic or engaging moments of Mad Men. *And I've noticed that* Mad Men *does have some of those. In fact, it has whole scenes that are boring, and which I struggle to understand the narrative point of. But I forgive that flabbiness in its scriptwriting, if that's what it is (maybe I simply don't understand the significance of those scenes), given the overall awesomeness of the series.*

In most scenes, during most dialogue, I was engaged, and I suppose my brain was not having other thoughts. And so to the last scene…

Betty Draper (Don Draper's wife) is talking to Helen Bishop, the mother of a young boy called Glen. Glen is in love with Betty and had run away from home; he'd been sleeping in the wooden house in the Drapers' garden. Betty discovered Glen in the wooden house (well, her dog did, actually) and brought him inside, cooked him a meal, and watched cartoons with him. Then, later, she called Helen, Glen's mother.

Helen picks Glen up. But later, maybe on another day, Helen comes round again to see Betty. She's angry with Betty. Betty says she hasn't done anything wrong, and says that Glen is lonely. They open up to each other. Betty says that her husband Don is not living at home anymore. They share their pain. There are silences.

And... well, this is when the peculiar thing happens. It's as if someone switches on the world. I hear the birds tweeting outside first; then distant traffic, and church bells ringing. Then I see the colours in the room. And the TV screen hovering on the wall in front of me, with beautiful moving pictures. And everything becomes 3D. And I feel that everything is OK. Beautiful, actually. I feel a deep sense of peace – I think that's what it is. Acceptance maybe. A kind of 'all is well in the world'.

And then Helen says, with a sigh – 'The hardest part... is realizing you're in charge.'

Her words blew me away. I realized that, just as I was sitting back watching the show – both Mad Men *and the show of life that had just erupted before me – I was effectively sitting back in life too. I realized that I'm not really in charge, and thus there isn't this 'hardest part'.*

And now, 40 minutes later, a car ticks over outside, then cuts as the engine is turned off. Then a door slams. And the birds tweet. And a chair is scraped over the floor in a nearby apartment. And a dog barks. Now, I still feel it. Somewhat dimmed, maybe, by the exercise of committing this to typed-out words.

In fact, in moving from the sofa to the sleeping laptop, and unsleeping it and opening a file to write this, and the file not opening, and all the Word documents saying they're 'not responding'... and staying patient and calm until the cursor finally started to flicker on the blank page – like someone slowly tapping their fingers on a table when waiting for something to happen or something to be said – there was the reminder to me of the world I can't control; or even my single rebelling billionth copy of Microsoft Office, or whatever package it is that Word is part of.

And now, as my neighbour sings, as she often does – it sounds more like humming today, actually – I contemplate the other times in my life that such powerful moments have occurred. The time I was meditating late at night, many years ago now, when I heard voices next door, and a quite distinct conversation going on. Then I realized it was my own thoughts.

And the time on the beach in 2002 when I had a huge feeling of energy at a point in my lower spine, like an energy gateway opening up. It was astonishing, and I didn't want the feeling to go away, but it did after a couple of minutes.

And all those moments of epiphany, of understanding. When everything is seen more clearly. When everything is felt more clearly. They come and they go.

*For me, 'awakening' is not a linear process, as some people suggest it can be. I have moments and periods of clarity. And when I do, I try to bring back some of what I've experienced into my everyday life. I bring back things in a variety of ways. 'F**k It' is one of those things, actually. F**k It is the feeling I get when I see clearly – when I see that everything's OK, and that things don't matter so much.*

I see this phenomenon in religions and spiritual traditions and philosophies. I see it as what people have tried to bring back from their experience of clarity. The thing is, we then get those things second-hand. And, because they're often not experienced or handled with such clarity, they then morph into something else; and once they're third-hand, they can be ugly things.

The invitation, though, is to try to use the 'things' that are brought back (by ourselves or others) to contact that experience first-hand. And that, I suppose, is what the title of this book I'm writing does. F**k It. Be At Peace with Life, Just As It Is *is a snapshot of reality taken from the space of clarity. It can therefore jar with our current view of reality ('How can I possibly be "at peace" with all this going on?'), or we can relax and let go and feel the message.*

And in doing so we can edge towards a wider view from the space of clarity ourselves. Or not even 'edge towards' sometimes. After all, one hour ago, it just happened to me. Out of the blue.

It's a little like being an astronaut. When they aren't at work, astronauts live a regular life as regular people with a regular view of the world, but when they get blasted into space, they're given a new and clear view of the planet they've been treading the whole of their lives.

They suddenly realize things about human existence that they hadn't realized before. For example, that we're all in this together – the human race – and that we should see this and work together more on our small planet.

They realize these things from the clarity of being in space, looking at Earth below. Then they return to Earth (and re-entry can be tough, and they risk being burned up and losing everything… I'm writing here, of course, with one eye on the metaphor. And they share with everyone what they saw from their (literal) space of clarity.

Along the way, since they experienced their moment of epiphany, astronauts have tried to capture their epiphanic moment in a variety of ways… usually in words, using those to try to convey that feeling or perception to themselves in as adequate a way as possible. And they bring those words back. Which are as a photograph taken of Earth from that spacecraft. They might have elements of accuracy, but they're not the real thing – they're not the true apprehension of the visual panorama or the enlightened perception.

And they share those words with the rest of the human race: maybe in press interviews, or in talks to high-school kids, or in books. And they do so for years, often decades, to come: the words changing slightly over time, drifting free a little or a lot from their original clarity.

Like the photograph fading. Until the words and the photograph become the thing itself. The original thing, over time, is replaced by the attempted recording of that thing.

And people, over the years, take the words and the photographs, and they place their own interpretations on them. They take the perception that 'we're all in this together' and draw up free trade agreements and nuclear proliferation treaties, and compose songs about equality and march for peace and write adverts for fizzy drinks that start with the words, 'I'd like to teach the world to sing.'

Some of these people, through the words and the photographs, access that clear perception and feeling. Others don't get beyond the words and photographs, and make their own thing of it entirely, laced with their skewed, non-space-clarity perceptions.

That, for me, as well as describing a common experience of space travel, describes a common experience of spiritual, religious, philosophical, artistic, psychological travel. We explore. We see clearly. We try to bring it back. And sometimes the medium we use (ideas, words, commandments on a stone, music, pictures) takes people there. And sometimes people take the medium we use to interpret in their own way, often twisting it for their own purposes.

And now, 100 minutes later, I still hear the birds tweeting, thunder rattling in the distance, people chatting on the street below, an aeroplane flying overhead. And it's time for that walk. Before the storm hits the shore of Fano, on the east coast of Italy, which is in southern Europe; a thigh-high boot kicking down towards North Africa – that huge continent that gets smaller as we see it as just some green against the blue of the sea as we see just a glowing blue planet in the distance.

The feeling of the experience I had in May 2017 faded somewhat over time, but it didn't disappear. I'd then occasionally experience the same level of perceptive intensity, again randomly. On one occasion (in June) I was driving on the motorway, and the same thing happened, in that I could suddenly hear and see everything in a more intense way. Then I noticed dozens of birds gathering overhead and then flying in the same direction as I was travelling – as if they were consciously accompanying me on my journey.

These experiences were apparently random. Sure, I practise Qigong every day, and I sit around a lot drinking tea (you know, by now, what that means), but no more than I'd usually do. More reliable evidence, though, for the importance of some form of regular (or, indeed, intense) peace practice, came during the Qigong retreat I taught on Stromboli this summer.

Now, before you start reading the following diary entry, it's worth saying that it describes the peak experience of the whole 'be at peace' process I went through while writing this book. We've discussed various ways of highlighting this section more. I quite fancied the idea that when the reader turned the page to begin reading this diary entry, a pop-up (paper or card) boxing glove would spring out and punch them in the face, to represent the consciousness-punching significance of this bit of the book.

Much discussion was had as to the risks a paper boxing glove might pose to a reader. And, given that I'm now warning you about the possibility of this before you turn the page, maybe we were advised that we could do it, as long as I wrote a warning on the preceding page.

Actually, as it so often does, it came down to a matter of cost, as well as health and safety. So the boxing-glove idea was another one that got away. And we were left with the much cheaper option of printing this section in ink mixed with the gland secretions of the *incilius alvarius* or Colorado River toad. We concluded that inhalation of the 5-MeO-DMT chemical-infused ink would enhance the effect of this revelatory section.

Please breathe out, and then turn the page.

Diary entry: 18 July 2017 – The Breeze of Peace

I'm running a Qigong retreat. And something big happened in the session this afternoon. It didn't announce itself as something big at the time. It just appeared as something very ordinary and everyday – but these things often do.

In fact, earlier in the week, I was talking about everyday epiphanies. I used the word 'epiphanic' for these experiences, and then wondered out loud if I'd made that word up. Well, I just looked up 'epiphanic' and it does exist, and this is what it means:

A sudden, intuitive perception of or insight into the reality or essential meaning of something – usually initiated by some simple, homely, or commonplace occurrence or experience.

So I was sitting there this afternoon in one of the comfy outdoor armchairs (did the chair have something to do with it?) and I was surfing between these states: some thoughts, then some watching, then lots of space, and lots of feeling the breeze and hearing the sounds.

And then I suddenly felt this sense of there being a space; maybe I thought this was my head at first, through which all of this was moving.

I know, it doesn't sound very 'big' does it? Bear with me, please. Let's see if it gets any better...

It was a new feeling, but a very natural feeling. There was this space, and the thoughts and the sounds and the feeling of the sunshine and any emotions or memories, or sights of the other people in the group, were all just gently blowing through this space, like the breeze from the sea below that was gently blowing through our seated group.

And, somehow, all those elements felt the same. The thoughts were the same as the sights were the same as the slight ache in my knee was the same as the buzz of the 'Ape' three-wheeled van whizzing round the alleyways.

As I felt this, I relaxed more and dropped back. I was also noticing this experience as I had it. I couldn't really tell where the space was either, and in a gentle way I was wondering, Is this in my brain cavity, or is it this space on the rooftop? Or is this a vast space – a universal-everything space – with things just blowing through?

Time was up too soon. I, like more than half the group now, could have sat for longer. But we shared – more deeply than we'd done before. Some people shared some difficult things, and I was touched by what people said. But something else was happening too: their words, insightful or painful, were just the same as the sound of the children playing on the beach, or the thoughts in my own head, or the breeze blowing in from the sea and through our group.

At the same time, I felt more moved by what people were saying – truly touched – but also utterly at peace with whatever they were saying. Not me being at peace with their words, or them, but just a sense of this big space, through which everything was blowing. And that was peaceful.

It was hard to convey in words, and still is, how profound that experience was. It was probably the most perception-altering experience I've had in my life. And it wasn't about 'understanding' anything: it was about 'feeling' something. It was more sensation than comprehension. And as such, it's very difficult to pass on.

Although, as before, the intensity of this sensation has faded, its residue has remained in my consciousness. It was a feeling that fundamentally shifted the way I feel; and, as a natural effect, the way I think. The assertion 'be at peace with life, just as it is' was felt, and then understood, completely clearly: then (and now).

F**K IT TO DOUBT

Neither you nor I can be sure of *your* precise route to a deep understanding and sense of this being-at-peace-with-life-just-as-it-is thing. I suspect it will involve a mix of practice (Level 2) and intellectual understanding (the theory of Level 3) that will then, in its own magical way, sprout the kind of apparently random epiphanic experiences that I've recounted here, and seen in others.

But if that leaves you with too much doubt and uncertainty, it's time to say F**k It to doubt, and for me to take you on a journey of neuroscientific discovery.

I've already mentioned that the Level 1 time-based procrastination of peacefulness is likely rooted in the brain's left hemisphere; and that the Level 2 present-based experience of peacefulness is rooted in the brain's right hemisphere. Level 3, then, is best described as a form of 'allowing of movement' between the two hemispheres, in a perfectly natural way.

But there's a neuroscientific insight that might allow you – with a degree of certainty – to comprehend the underlying and sometimes overriding sensation of being at peace, with life, just as it is.

This insight was most persuasively and dramatically experienced and then recounted by American Jill Bolte Taylor in her book *My Stroke of Insight*. Bolte Taylor was, and is, a neuroanatomist, and thus has a profound understanding of how the brain works.

On 10 December 1996, when she was 37 years old, Bolte Taylor woke up feeling unwell. As she got moving, and attempted to make herself feel better (she did some exercise, started to run a bath and so on), she began to realize that something was seriously wrong. And, as the symptoms accumulated, she realized she was having a stroke.

She was rapidly losing the ability to walk, talk, read, and remember numbers (for making an emergency telephone call), or to recall anything of her life, for that matter. Yet, while this catastrophic brain haemorrhage was happening, she experienced a huge sense of peace. A sense of peace that she'd never before experienced in her life: a sense that everything was fine as it was (even though, at another level in her brain, she knew that she could be dying).

After a long struggle to recall the right phone number, Bolte Taylor managed to call for help. She was rushed to hospital, and over the following eight years, she did recover from the stroke. But the huge insight that the stroke elicited was that, as she puts it:

'Peace is only a thought away, and all we have to do to access it is silence the voice of our dominating left mind.'

Bolte Taylor knew this because her left brain had been forcibly silenced, and she'd then been dropped into such an overwhelming sense of peace.

Peace, then, is not somewhere else (as we think in Level 1). It's available here and now (Level 2): it's just that the noise of the left brain drowns out the quiet peace of the right brain.

Indeed, there are many stories in various spiritual traditions of the treasure that's searched for, far and wide, and then discovered, in the end, at home: right under the noses of the seekers. The moral of all these stories is that 'it was there all along, and it is, thus, here now'.

Underneath the noise of everything, is peace. The default mode is peace. It's the foundation. It's what our brain returns to when the rest subsides. It's not that, when we don't appear to be at peace, the peace disappears. It's always there.

And that's the insight that can eliminate the doubt that you'll access the at-peace thing. In this moment you are, underneath it all, at peace. There's a part of your brain that knows everything's fine – not that it'll be fine if certain conditions are met, and certain things turn out in certain ways. But that, whatever happens, everything is fine, and OK just as it is.

Another person who had the same insight as a result of severe ill health was the 14th-century English Christian mystic Julian of Norwich. She – yes she – had powerful spiritual visions during her illness (and she was so ill, she was given the last rites). Later, she wrote about them in her *Revelations of Divine Love* (the first book in the English language known to have been written by a woman). These are the most famous words from that book:

'All shall be well, and all shall be well,
and all manner of things shall be well.'

Now this might also be the first example of the rhetorical trick of repeating a word or phrase three times to emphasize the point: such as when you're told that the three most important things in setting up a shop are 'location, location, location', or when former British prime minister Tony Blair set out his priorities as 'education, education, education'.

Julian of Norwich could have summed up her insight like this: 'The most important thing I realized was that all shall be well.' But she says 'shall be well' twice, for effect. And then, as if the word 'all' isn't clear enough, she says 'all manner of things' and goes for a third strike.

It's the knowledge of this, as fact – taken either from a 14th-century mystic, or a 21st-century neuroanatomist, or from your own epiphanic moments – that can eliminate any doubt and provide you with a Level 3 understanding of the whole at-peace thing. Namely, even when you don't feel at peace – and the world and your life feel anything but – you are, underneath, at peace.

Now, I'm guessing that as you contemplate all this, questions will come up (from your left brain, probably). So, I can switch off the Powerpoint presentation now and open to questions...

I'm really struggling at the moment.
How can I feel this sense of being 'at peace'?

A:

F**K IT. BE AT PEACE WITH DIFFICULTY

You can try to work with relaxing and attempting to feel at peace in the moment. It depends on the level of struggle, the nature of your difficulty, and how agitated you are. Many people get great results from practices such as meditation or gratitude in times of difficulty. They are about working with your response to whatever is difficult. Of course, you can also try to work with the source of your difficulty. What can you do, if anything, to reduce the cause of the difficulty?

In both ways of dealing with difficulty – dealing with the source and dealing with your response – you're likely to experience fluctuating levels of stress, and at least some peace. The breakthrough comes when you realize that beneath it all, a part of you is already at peace – that everything is actually fine as it is, and that everything will turn out for the best. It's the remembering of this that adds a new quality to the struggle.

That new quality isn't perpetual peace – that would be crazy, given the circumstances – but it's a holding of the struggle within a new, benign context. The shift, then, is in the background – and that might, or might not, affect the local, everyday experience.

Q:

What about injustice – how can we
possibly be at peace with that?

A:

F**K IT. BE AT PEACE
WITH INJUSTICE

The world is not just. Whether we see the manifestation of this on the
news every day, or we directly experience injustice personally (and
painfully), we can't start with the assumption that the world should
be just (because it isn't), or live in the hope of it becoming just (it
won't).

We have to deal with injustice. We can thus fight it, and attempt to
win through. And many brave people have made the world a better
place for us all by fighting injustice. Or, if we can't fight it, we have to
deal with it another way.

Religious people might suggest that forgiveness is the only way to be
at peace around injustice. But attempts at forgiveness can deny our
natural anger. To be at peace with our own anger around injustice is

the most likely route to clearing such anger – and, one day maybe, feeling at peace about the actual situation.

So, remembering our underlying at-peace nature doesn't exclude or banish the fight or the anger; instead it's the opposite: it includes all. Full stop.

Q:
How can I get through this stress
and anxiety to feeling at peace?

A:
F**K IT. BE AT PEACE WITH STRESS AND ANXIETY

From the perspective of a stressed or anxious self, the idea of being at peace feels like the far-off promised land. There are many valid ways and techniques for dealing with, and thus reducing, levels of stress and anxiety (some of which I've outlined in this book, such as 'sitting and drinking tea').

But both stress and anxiety should not simply be seen as 'wrong' and therefore something to be eliminated. Our stress response is an essential survival response and we'd never want to train it out of ourselves.

Of course, stress and anxiety can be debilitating in the present, and detrimental to our health in the long term, but they are simple feedback mechanisms that invite us to look at our lives and make changes. It's best to see stress as a helpful warning flag that's trying to tell you something – you just have to get your warning flag manual out and look up the meaning.

This rational understanding of stress is also a step in the direction of the full acceptance of the stress and anxiety that exists at your underlying at-peace level, which is always there, in the background. So being 'at peace' with stress and anxiety means, as it suggests, not an elimination of either, but a gentle acceptance of both.

That is life, after all. For most of us, stress and even anxiety are a part of life. We can (on the one hand) work with the sources and our responses, but (on the other hand) we can sit back into an acceptance of them, too.

I'm obsessed with what I've done wrong, and
my failures. How can I find some peace?

A:

F**K IT. BE AT PEACE
WITH FAILURE

Google the term 'failure quotes' and you'll soon feel better. I love the
following one by Winston Churchill (please imagine him saying this
as you read it):

'Success is the ability to go from one failure
to another with no loss of enthusiasm.'

In this era of relentless Facebook friends' status updates, it's easy
to think that everyone's doing well and is happy. It's less tempting to
post a photo of the bus stop in the rain than one of the beach; or a
shot of your disappointing exam results than your top grades; or your
tired and down selfie than your made-up and cheery self.

Look up 'CV of failures' too. One professor at the prestigious
Princeton University in the USA published a CV of all his failures,
and got more publicity for that than he ever did for his successful

academic work. The failures included degree programmes he hadn't got onto, research funding he hadn't got, and paper rejections from academic journals.

We *all* fail. It's just that most of us keep quiet about these failures. When we're feeling down about our failures, and we look around us, all we see is people singing about their successes. So we assume that's all there is.

Even at this rational level then, I can start to feel at peace with my failures. But if you drop to the underlying at-peace level, there is no recognition of something as a 'failure' at all. There's just life being lived, and things being experienced. There's not the colour of judgement, only the technicolour of a full and vivid life – unfolding moment to moment like a miracle.

Q:
How could I ever be at peace
with those who've hurt me?

A:
F**K IT. BE AT PEACE
WITH HURTFUL PEOPLE

F**k 'em, the bastards. People can be cruel and hurtful and sometimes pure wicked. And it's even harder when you've trusted them, and confided in them, and given them so much. That they could then be so cruel and hurtful in return – F**k 'em.

Sure, you can conjecture that whatever happened to them while they were growing up was difficult for them. Or maybe you can see that they didn't understand what they were doing. But it doesn't alter the fact that they were cruel and hurtful to you. You can't forgive and you're unlikely to forget. And you're tired of people telling you that you need to let it go.

So... feel it. Don't feel guilty that you still feel like this. You feel the way you do, and that's that. The only way it will ever pass is for you to stop blocking yourself when you feel it (with thoughts like, *Oh, I should have let go of this by now*).

Being at peace with hurtful people, then, is to recognize that there will always be some hurtful people out there; and to fully feel the pain when they hurt us. As the biggest hurt they could cause is locking inside us any unexpressed pain.

I've just lost someone close unexpectedly.
How can I feel at peace with that?

A:

F**K IT. BE AT PEACE WITH BAD THINGS HAPPENING

A part of all of us sits coiled up in dread at the possibility of bad things happening. Our very nervous system is constantly on the lookout for the first signs of the threat and the bad thing.

And bad things *do* happen, clearly. Bad things are likely to happen to me, and to you. Bad things have happened to me, and likely to you too. And the bad things that have happened, which you and I have survived, sometimes make us stronger, and sometimes make us weaker and more scared about more bad things happening again.

I really wouldn't want a replay of certain things I've experienced. My gut tightens up if I just flash a few of them through my mind. Rationally, I'm partially reassured by the fact that, like most people, I'm likely to get through the bad things that happen. We seem to have a way of getting through and surviving the most difficult of circumstances.

Though I find it hard to imagine now how I'd get through certain scenarios that I don't even want to imagine today, experience (my own, and of seeing others) tells me that it's possible.

Rationally, I know that bad things happen. And that it's a part of life. Bad things are happening to people every day. But to have a rational stance on such bad things is a long way off feeling 'at peace' with them. I'd have to drop a whole lot of attachments, and say some huge 'F**k Its', to get close to that.

But I don't need to do that. Because I know that, underneath, there's the understanding that, whatever happens in life, all shall be well. And this 'all shall be well' voice is like the calming tones of a parent reassuring their frightened child. The parent knows that, in the context of the thing the child is worrying about, everything will be OK. And this voice knows that, in the context of everything our earthly mind and meat-suit can face, everything will be OK.

Q:

This constant news about President Trump and North Korea is freaking me out. How can I be at peace with the possibility of nuclear annihilation?

A:

F**K IT. BE AT PEACE WITH THE BOMB

As you know from the many references made to it in this book, I've spent this year, 2017, very aware, and disturbed, by the escalating tensions between North Korea and the USA.

I've asked many people, most of whom don't seem as concerned as I've been, how they've been able to process the news. And they invariably say the same thing: 'Oh, I don't watch the news anymore.' They then give a reason for that, such as, 'It's always the same negative stuff' or 'It's just politicians saying the same thing, and they're all the same anyway'. Or, without any irony, given the likely source of this perception: 'Well, the news is all fake anyway.' For these people, ignorance is bliss, or at least the normality of everyday life.

You could argue that they've found their peace with it, but that it's an 'it' they don't understand and refuse to hear anything about. And this may be a rational and healthy response, given that there's little or nothing we can do to help avert a nuclear war.

(I didn't want to write just 'nothing' there, as I'm sure you could find a way to argue that if we voted for him or her, or lobbied for this or that, or marched here or there, it could conceivably have an effect);

And there's little or nothing we can do to prepare for such an eventuality – in any way that would make a difference – come that eventuality. (Again, I'm allowing for the bunker-with-water-and-food-stocks preparation stance that some will take here.)

Given this, then, why get all het up as we pore over the horrific possibilities of something we can't do anything about? Best to play the finest tune on your violin as the *Titanic* goes down, without paying much attention to the *Titanic* going down.

But to me, the most rational response, initially at least, is fear and horror (which has the same rhetorical ring, funnily enough, as Trump's 'fire and fury'). We're facing the possibility of an escalating nuclear war… of the apocalypse. Please allow me to get scared, upset and a bit teary about the potentially huge loss of human life, the vast scale of the suffering, and the annihilation of life as we know it.

You'll know by now that at Level 3 at-peace-training, we don't exclude that response, or avoid it, or suppress it. It's the most natural response. But there's one unavoidable fact about this whole crisis: it's *happening*. We don't know, at this point in time, where it will go (though I'm guessing Trump has some pretty clear ideas already), but it's happening.

This crisis, like the health issue you have, and the noisy neighbours who keep you up at night, and your money worries, and the way young people talk to each other nowadays – and every other aspect of life that seems to stop you feeling at peace – *is happening*.

And yet, underneath all those fearful, anxious, angry, exasperated thoughts, is the thought and perception that 'all shall be well'. Even in the most extreme not-being-well scenario, there's a bit of us thinking, feeling and knowing that all shall be well.

There's a bit of us that is at peace with the bomb. And to be at peace with something, and with everything – with life, as it is – doesn't exclude all that is *not* peace: instead, it includes and even embraces all of it.

That's truly what being at peace means. It's about the most radical thing you can imagine. It includes all that is not apparently at peace, calm in the knowledge that all there is, is peace.

There's a book that refers to 'the peace ... which passeth all understanding...'.[4] I think this is meant as a rhetorical device, a form of hyperbole that's actually saying, 'This kind of peace is not what you think it is, and it's really rather difficult to understand.' If it were literal, we'd be lost, and it would become like a Zen Buddhist kōan or some missive from a pretentious, exclusive club of a 'If you think you understand x, then you haven't understood it' nature.

I mention it though because understanding this at-peace thing is clearly not easy: it has to be felt as much as understood; and both the feeling and the understanding of it will come and go. That, it seems, is also life, as it is.

---

4 The book is the Bible, and specifically, Philippians 4:7 of that book.

POSTSCRIPT

The title of this book – *F**k It. Be at Peace with Life, Just as It Is* – is in the second person. I, the author, am suggesting that you could be at peace with life, just as it is.

Yet the epiphanic experiences that happened to me during the writing of this book were characterized by the feeling of an absence of the 'I', the 'you', and all the other personal pronouns. There's just the breezing-in of stuff, non-differentiated – so the traffic noise has as much value as the voice of pain, and neither seem tethered to anything else.

Sure, the personal pronouns come back in, all the time. I reappear as me, and you reappear as you. But they seem to have been found out, too. I don't get into it much – the possibility that the 'me' thing is a delusion or a construct – because I'm unlikely to be able to persuade myself that I don't exist. But there's something there that sees my 'I' as much and as little a part of the game as my big toe or a Big Mac or the Big Apple.

And this feels like the end of the film that leaves an opening for the next. And it usually involves the hint that a character you thought was dead is still very much alive. This ending, on the contrary, involves the hint that a character you thought was alive is not there at all, and maybe never has been.

Evil laughter, starting low and getting higher, and then fading away into the distance.

With thanks to, in particular –
Michelle Pilley

Dedicated to, in particular –
Patrick Lucocq, 1966–2018
Friend and an original F**kiteer

ABOUT THE AUTHOR

Gaia Pollini

John C. Parkin, the son of Anglican preachers, realized that saying 'F**k It' was as powerful as the Eastern philosophical practices he'd been studying for 20 years.

John and his wife, Gaia, had already said F**k It to media jobs in London and escaped to Italy with their twin baby boys in 2002 to set up a meditation and retreat centre. They were soon teaching F**k It retreats, and the first F**k It book (F**k It: The Ultimate Spiritual Way) was written in a frenzy of F**k It excitement in 2005.

The F**k It word(s) spread quickly all over the world.

Since then – through this bestselling series of F**k It books, F**k It retreats around the world and online courses and memberships – John and Gaia have inspired hundreds of thousands of people to worry less and live more.

They spend their days sharing the power of saying F**k It, walking by the sea and eating gelato.

www.thefuckitlife.com

JOIN THE F**K IT AUTHORS IN PERSON IN ITALY FOR A F**K IT RETREAT

This is where it all started: John & Gaia ran their first F**k It Retreat in 2005.
They run these famous retreats in spectacular locations around Italy, including
on the live volcano of Stromboli, on the beach of Pesaro and in a luxury spa near
Urbino.
*Say F**k It and treat yourself to a F**k It Retreat.*

'Anything that helps you let go is okay on a F**k It Retreat.' THE OBSERVER
'I witnessed some remarkable transformations during my F**k It Retreat.' KINDRED SPIRIT

LIVE THE F**K IT LIFE   WWW.THEFUCKITLIFE.COM

We hope you enjoyed this Hay House book. If you'd like to receive our online catalog featuring additional information on Hay House books and products, or if you'd like to find out more about the Hay Foundation, please contact:

Hay House, Inc., P.O. Box 5100, Carlsbad, CA 92018-5100
(760) 431-7695 or (800) 654-5126
(760) 431-6948 (fax) or (800) 650-5115 (fax)
www.hayhouse.com® • www.hayfoundation.org

———

Published in Australia by: Hay House Australia Pty. Ltd.,
18/36 Ralph St., Alexandria NSW 2015
Phone: 612-9669-4299 • *Fax:* 612-9669-4144
www.hayhouse.com.au

Published in the United Kingdom by: Hay House UK, Ltd.,
The Sixth Floor, Watson House, 54 Baker Street, London W1U 7BU
Phone: +44 (0)20 3927 7290 • *Fax:* +44 (0)20 3927 7291
www.hayhouse.co.uk

Published in India by: Hay House Publishers India,
Muskaan Complex, Plot No. 3, B-2, Vasant Kunj, New Delhi 110 070
Phone: 91-11-4176-1620 • *Fax:* 91-11-4176-1630
www.hayhouse.co.in

———

Access New Knowledge.
Anytime. Anywhere.

Learn and evolve at your own pace
with the world's leading experts.

www.havhouseU.com